transformation in action. For faith-rooted leaders, her theological connections to creating, creation, and the created, set within the hospitality practices of Gates, offer community activists ways to engage in art and the public in an embodied way that lends itself to the spiritual encounters of both the Divine and neighbors. I am thankful to Fee for lifting up the work of Gates as a theological practice that pushes and challenges the way in which we see and dwell in our neighborhoods.

—Joyce del Rosario, director of multiethnic programs,
Seattle Pacific University

The work of Theaster Gates defies straightforward categorization, and his determination to have an impact beyond the borders of the contemporary artworld have made him an irrepressible voice for clarity, wisdom, and healing more broadly. Maria Fee's illuminating text provides the fullest, most holistic account yet of the richly theological connections issuing from Gates's profound efforts to renew land, labor, and community. She sets out a feast of insight and reflection that demonstrates how theologians might do justice to the far-reaching scope of Gates's distinctive vision and at the same time amplify the good of his work themselves.

—Taylor Worley, visiting associate professor of art history,
Wheaton College

Praise for *Beauty Is a Basic Service*

Only an artist, pastor, theologian, and mentor like Maria Fee could present the work of Black performance artist Theaster Gates with such grace and wisdom. Her claim is bold: Gates's art of place-making—of curating places and material things in ways that reflect God's own hospitality—may serve as a model for reimagining Christian belief and practice in a secular age. The result is one of the best examples of practical theology I've read in a long time.

—William Dyrness, senior professor of theology and culture, Fuller Theological Seminary; author of *The Facts on the Ground: A Wisdom Theology of Culture*

Maria Fee's *Beauty Is a Basic Service* confirms Theaster Gates as one of the most significant artists of his generation, and this book, diligently and sensitively written, is a landmark achievement for our "art+faith" conversation. Fee is a first-rate artist who has served in the long and daunting journey of serving the church and, in her long-suffering, has nurtured her "theology of hospitality" generatively, invoking the new creation.

—Makoto Fujimura, artist and author of *Art and Faith: A Theology of Making*

In *Beauty Is a Basic Service*, Dr. Maria Fee models the theology of hospitality that she also locates in the work of Theaster Gates. Weaving together multiple theological traditions, art criticism, and art history with evocative, careful description, Fee offers an accessible, substantial, joyful introduction to Gates's community-oriented practice. Fee helps us see how Gates's work can be *both* critical of broken systems and generous in its love, calling on all readers—whether scholars, makers, or curious viewers—to do the same.

—Dr. Elissa Yukiko Weichbrodt, associate professor of art and art history, Covenant College, and author of *Redeeming Vision: A Christian Guide to Looking at and Learning from Art*

It is believed that the greatest gift one can offer is one's life. I see Maria Fee's book, *Beauty Is a Basic Service*, as one of those rare gifts that cannot be contained on a shelf or placed on a table in the living room. *Beauty Is a Basic Service* is a feast of good news. Fee compels us to look at our Christian walk more soberly by interrogating our "theology of hospitality" through the life work of social practice artist Theaster Gates. Her book takes us on a spiritual journey, and along the way she challenges Protestant belief structures and Christian dogma, and deconstructs these towers of faith systems that blind our vision of the full body of the kingdom. In the end she brings us to a place where we can see the "other" without fear drenched in stereotypic constructions, but through a lens of love, compassion, and understanding. This book beckons us to honestly see ourselves in a mirror, acknowledging the beauty within, and to offer thanks to the Peerless One who created us.

—Steve A. Prince, director of engagement and distinguished artist in residence at the Muscarelle Museum of Art at William & Mary University

Through this insightful introduction to the work of artist Theaster Gates, Maria Fee reveals the ways art can make a place for God to dwell in moments of human making and community life. Fee invites readers into a theological reflection on hospitality in an age when we need it most, and does so through the embodied spirituality that only the arts can cultivate. Readers will come away challenged in how they understand their own practices in place and encouraged in the hospitable work of the Holy Spirit in the material world.

—Jennifer Allen Craft, associate professor of theology and humanities, Point University, and author of *Placemaking and the Arts: Cultivating the Christian Life*

Maria Fee's focus on the life and work of Theaster Gates has expanded my imagination and understanding of how to approach social

BEAUTY Is a BASIC SERVICE

BEAUTY IS A BASIC SERVICE

Theology and Hospitality in the Work of

THEASTER GATES

MARIA FEE

FORTRESS PRESS
MINNEAPOLIS

BEAUTY IS A BASIC SERVICE
Theology and Hospitality in the Work of Theaster Gates

Cover design: Kristin Miller
Interior ink illustrations: Walker G. Fee

Print ISBN: 978-1-5064-6984-3
eBook ISBN: 978-1-5064-6985-0

In honor of Maudine Fee, and to her son, Brian Fee.
You both represent the ways creative endeavors confront the
agitations and dramas of this world. Thank you for the
steady reminder that art matters for God's sake.

Contents

Preface

The work of social practice installation artist and Chicago native Theaster Gates assists in the exploration of the aesthetic and theological dimensions of hospitality, specifically concerning place, people, and material things deemed unimportant. Through analysis of his poetic labor, one can see a theology of hospitality that amplifies God's care for the world and everything in it. In other words, Gates's hospitality shines a light on divine hospitality—the embrace of what is other.

By way of art comprised of nontraditional mediums like neighborhoods, gospel performances, and meal gatherings, Gates addresses personal corresponding experiences. His place-making labors that improve neglected neighborhoods hearken back to my urban upbringing. Gates's focus on race assists me in regarding the world from my complex identity as a Cuban American. As an artist and theologian, I admire the ways Gates moves beyond the disinterested confines of a Western philosophical tradition to re-associate[1] the social and spiritual value of art, without diminishing aesthetic satisfaction or integrity.

The just dimensions of the artist's work are personally gratifying as he tackles the discrepancies associated with being poor, urban, and a person of color. Siding with the disenfranchised, Gates elevates a vast and complex Black cultural heritage, which has been generally disparaged. Consequently, his testimony paves the way for this exploration of hospitality established in response to attitudes that disregard much of God's creation. As a woman, a minority, and an artist, I notice that for a great many Protestants (I speak from an evangelical and Reformed Protestant tradition), it is difficult to accommodate the physical world, including the body, into daily faith practices. Acquainted with faith systems that emphasize a command of thought and will, I have seen the ways the people of God mistrust what they deem as irrational or undisciplined. That which does not fit within strict dogmatic guidelines is considered suspect. Hence, the many attributes and dramas of real-life situations are discounted.

Theologian Gesa Elsbeth Thiessen contends that such incongruities are generated by a Christian theological anthropology that fears the material, sensual, and idolatrous. Thiessen relates how such suspicions have specifically affected three areas, "the perception of the senses, the role of the body, and the view of women."[2] Having worked under the province of a conservative denomination that perpetuates (white) male superiority, I concur with her insights. However, it should be noted that Thiessen has overlooked the problematic yet also physical realities of race and ethnicity. The research for this project commenced in 2015, the same year as the Charleston massacre at Emanuel African Methodist Episcopal Church. While I have been writing this book, there have been successive Black fatalities at the hands of police officers, the heated activist proceedings on athletic fields by Colin Kaepernick and others, the Black Lives Matter and Me Too movements, restrictive immigration policies, and the rise of hate crimes against the Asian community inflamed by the COVID-19 pandemic, resulting in the 2021 massage parlor shooting of Asian workers near Atlanta. The theological task became a form of lament, a way to make sense of inhospitable situations.

Theology is a human endeavor. Divorced from the body or circumstances, it tends to remain in the sphere of fixed ideas and theories. Such detachment can dehumanize. It gives Christians license to sideline situations concerning women, the gender fluid, minorities, immigrants, and artists. As an artist reacting to concrete reality, I am suspicious of Christian theological assertions that do not take into account the difficulties experienced by a great many people when trying to fulfill or accede to its tenets.[3] Rooted in the complex dramas of this world, I turn to artful theology. The realm of aesthetics substantially connects theology's mental preoccupations with external conditions. Accordingly, I view Gates as a prophet who communicates God's message written in the vein of Ezekiel-type performances that reveal divine dissatisfaction with Christianity's disregard of place, people, and material things. Faith is not solely dependent on the intellectual adoption of doctrines but must also physically engage the multivalent structures of God's world.[4] To this end, the art of Theaster Gates provides home-making methods for Christians, and in fact all people, to move beyond fear of being contaminated by the world to honoring its beauty and brokenness.

This study is an introduction to the social-based art of Theaster Gates, employed to better comprehend God's home-making activities. Three specific qualities of God's hospitality are emphasized and explored here, which also operate as a framework to construct a theology of hospitality. The first is the triune God's promise to care for creation. The second speaks of divine coherence; all things are organized in interrelated fashion, binding together creation and culture. And lastly, there is the spiritual dimension of hospitality. The Spirit of God employs an animating function to revive place, people, and things. This specific set of qualities has evolved from extensive exploration of the artworks and lectures of Theaster Gates.

Gates embodies and models the stewarding, reconciling, and vivifying modes of hospitality. Each chapter presents these qualities as Gates incarnates his belief through art strategies that display the viability of place (chapter 1), people (chapter 2), and material things (chapter 3). I analyze his work with artistic-social commentary, followed by a theological reflection that constructs a theology of hospitality to subsequently engender home-making habits within God's created order.

Gates provides adequate artistic resources for critical exploration, further eliciting concomitant praxis of hospitality. His art also presents a fresh reframing of the Scriptures and certain Christian traditions obscured by Western patterns of detachment.[5] Granted this artistic approach, Gates's construction of appealing localities mediating social rapport fosters a vital perception of God as favorable host. This inviting image intimately links God to creation, thereby accommodating the possibility for human–divine interactions. It also provides a reason to visit Gates's neighborhood, which discloses ideas and actions to prompt the renewal of Christian hospitality.

1

Hospitality and Place: The Dorchester Project

"What if I understood the sacredness of the city and that it is manifested through the things that I make?"

—Theaster Gates[1]

How does an undistinguished space become a *place*? Specifically, what are the inhabited practices, or the effective considerate acts that validate and realize *place*?[2] There is a simple feat—walking—used as a spatial measurement to animate place.[3] Adopting this ambulatory device, a stroll through Theaster Gates's Dorchester Project provides a method to not only apprehend his radical hospitality but also inspire others to generate similar deeds as a means to ratify place. Gates performs the idea where physical interactions with a locality become contracts signed by gestures, which subsequently transform general notions of space into dedicated habitations. If walking is understood as "the space of enunciation,"[4] then perhaps Gates's urban remodeling program is the *place of declaration*, expounding on the viability of poor neighborhoods.

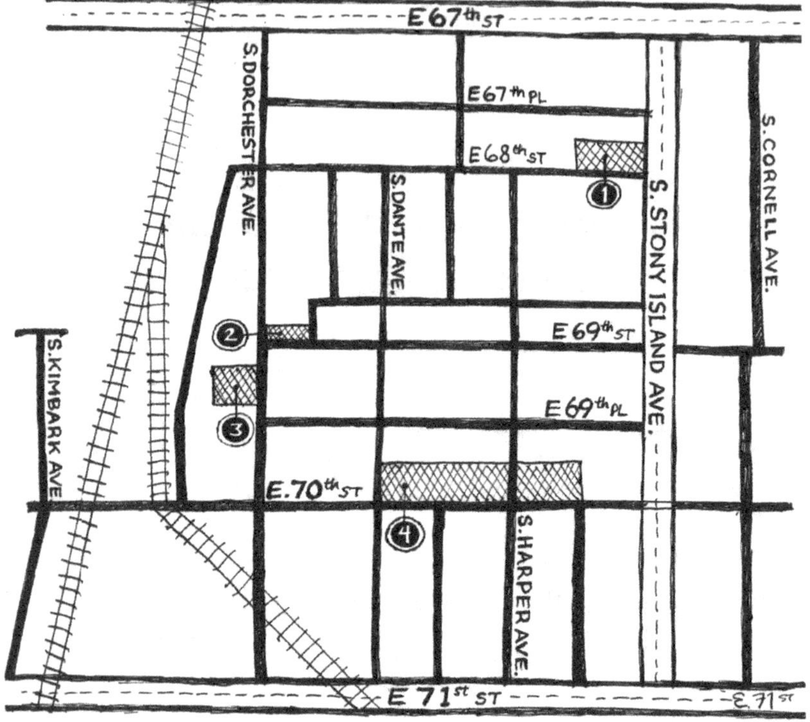

Figure 1.1. Map of a section of Greater Grand Crossings: 1. Stony Island Arts Bank. 2. The first Black Cinema House. 3. The Archive House and the Listening House. 4. Dorchester Housing + Art Collaborative.

THE DORCHESTER PROJECT

The Dorchester Project, which revamps abandoned buildings into cultural venues in his South Side of Chicago neighborhood of Greater Grand Crossings, best showcases Theaster Gates's redevelopment efforts.[5] This socio-spatial-durational art practice extends an invitation for all to enter into one of Chicago's struggling neighborhoods to partake in its poetic worth. Accepting the offer, we commence the mapped-out Dorchester Project Walking Tour (see figure 1.1), first, to enjoy Gates's home-making endeavors, and second, to blaze a path that correlates God's hosting practices with human social enterprises. This art and theology analysis further presents Gates's tactics as a basis for renewal of true Christian hospitality.

The excursion begins at Gates's first real-estate purchase, a formerly abandoned property at 6918 South Dorchester Avenue. Once a candy store, notable for its two transom-like windows, in Gates's hands, it originally functioned as a home and studio. Hired in 2006 as the University of Chicago's arts programmer, Gates resolved to set up house in one of the languishing Black neighborhoods nearby. Taking out loans, he purchased the candy store for $13,000. Afterward, Gates bought the vacant house next door for $16,000. The first property eventually evolved into the Listening House, where 8,000 albums retrieved from the closing of a Dr. Wax Records Shop were made accessible to musicians and music lovers alike. A DJ's delight, the space hosted vibrant gatherings focused on music prior to the opening of a larger setting at the Stony Island Arts Bank in 2015, also a tour destination.

Just two steps away is the second purchased property—the Archive House. It held a multimedia library that included the glass slides from the University of Chicago's art history department, and architectural books from the now-defunct Prairie Avenue Books. These items, along with the vinyl records, are now maintained at the Stony Island Arts Bank. The Archive House served as the site for Gates's *Soul Food Pavilion* dinners to be discussed in a later chapter. This two-story structure is typical of other homes on the block, except here, true to Gates's spirited vibe, long wooden planks are vertically placed as exterior siding. Such positioning draws the eye heavenward, while the warmth of the salvaged wood speaks of a revivalist mission ready to reach the souls of neighbors. The reclamation of materials and property serve to inspire and challenge others on the block to similarly reform their tired homes through resourceful means.

Crossing the street, we encounter 6901 South Dorchester Avenue, which housed the first incarnation of Black Cinema House but now functions solely as the artist's private residence. The vibrancy of

Black Cinema House's educational and film programming necessitated a move to a larger venue a few blocks down, at 7200 South Kimbark Avenue. Originally the Anheuser-Busch distribution warehouse, the Kimbark building not only hosts public viewings of films related to the Black diaspora but a portion of the structure also serves as Gates's studio. And, because he is a potter, an outdoor kiln sits in the yard.

Going back to the first Black Cinema House at 6901 South Dorchester Avenue, it is easy to admire the stately corner beauty with a remarkable, large circular window on the long side of the house, and a fancy Victorian-style, boxed corner window perch that juts out from the second floor. Before its restoration, salvaged architectural elements of this residence were shipped to Germany and entered into a visual and historical conversation with the Huguenot House at dOCUMENTA (13). This gave voice to Black and French Huguenot migrations and their alienation that necessitated recuperative hospitality.[6] Note that all these properties are titled *Houses*. They at one time or another functioned as both private abodes and as social hot-spots. Former artist-residents, including Gates, maintained an organic open-door policy that converted their living-working areas into public venues.[7] These dwellings served as cultural sanctuaries for media and people alike, thus blurring lines between public and private. Such turning inside-out of home opens a new format for carrying out hospitality where art plays host.

There are actual homes to be seen on this tour. In order to get to the Dorchester Art + Housing Collaborative, we walk past a middle school, catching an earful of youthful voices that break the quiet of the street. The neighborhood is tidy, yet wears a layer of fatigue, with its sinking porches, rusting fences, and long-grass yards. Dorchester Art + Housing Collaborative provides a fresh contrast, with its cut lawns and simple landscaping that hug the Bauhaus-style row houses. The plantings' muted greens and ochres further complement the serious nature of the red-brick structures, while the painted mustard color of the exterior doors draws us into its inner courts. By converting the abandoned city housing units into actual homes, Gates's aesthetic place-making activity amplifies his home-making tendencies.

Walking a couple of blocks north from the housing project, on traffic-heavy Stony Island Avenue, we approach the Stony Island State Bank, a grand Classical Revival edifice, now renamed Stony Island Arts Bank. It contains an art gallery, a tearoom, and a library, and houses multiple artifact collections. Built in 1923, the three-story-high pillared facade references a more prosperous era, when fancy commercial and entertainment establishments stood adjacent. In recent decades, the bank stood empty and served only as a visual landmark in the mental maps of Chicagoans driving by on the way to somewhere else. By reclaiming and restoring the abandoned structure, Gates has transformed the building into a destination.

This cultural flurry is employed in Grand Crossings, a place where 25 percent of the population lives below the poverty line. The flight of the middle class from such neighborhoods prompts Gates's question concerning stewardship of locality: "Is it possible to stay in a place and demonstrate a transformation in the quality of life by simply being artful in that place?"[8] This query looks to arouse fidelity to a type of habitation that encompasses the biblical concept of land management to be discussed later. Through conscientious labor of care and conservancy, Gates mirrors God's commitment to place, which subsequently administers life-giving properties to others.

As a result of the establishment of the nonprofit Rebuild Foundation, Gates's building momentum grew. Through artist-led ventures, Rebuild Foundation creates programs for and maintains the Grand Crossings sites. What is more, the Dorchester Project becomes paradigmatic for Rebuild's ventures in other cities.[9] "I am keen on ensuring that more folk have access to the amazing cultural experiences that I have access to," declares Gates.[10] Rebuild also operates as a laboratory for the University of Chicago initiative

Arts Incubator and Art + Public Life, of which Gates is the director. This consists of an arts center, artist residencies, neighborhood art programming, and a restaurant just west of Washington Park. These happenings are tangible proof of an aesthetic-ethical neighborliness, otherwise known as hospitality. Hospitality as an art form honors *dwelling* as a mode of aesthetic contemplation, the potentiality of neglected neighborhoods, and the communal as an arena for transformation.

THE HOST: THEASTER GATES

To better grasp the artistic, social, and place-specific dimensions of Theaster Gates's work, let's turn to the fall of 1968. Some five years before Gates's birth in 1973, a cultural collaboration formed in Chicago's West Side from the inspired energies of the Black Arts movement, the desire for innovative programming by the Museum of Contemporary Art (MCA) in Chicago, and the concerns of former street gang members regarding ghetto life conditions. These forces combined resources to bring about the experimental Art & Soul culture center on Sixteenth Street in North Lawndale. The center offered short-term studio space for artists, provided materials, books, and classes for the community, and served as a neighborhood gathering spot, hosting poetry readings and concerts. Unlike the art-world trend of the time known as Happenings,[11] Art & Soul's innovative programming derived from a Black notion of art that did not stray far from the social, political, spiritual, and quotidian needs of its community.[12] Indeed, the Black Arts movement promulgated a racial aesthetic encompassing Black social life energized by an Afro-centric awareness following the dismantling of European colonialism, the contributions of the civil rights movement, and the growing number of Black studies programs.[13] This identity-racial aesthetic is a root of the artwork of Theaster Gates.

Art & Soul, then, personifies the Black consciousness present in Gates's early life, laden with aesthetic and social-activist aspirations. The close geographic proximity of Art & Soul to Gates's childhood neighborhood in East Garfield Park is not coincidental. Gates also worked at a similar nonprofit arts education center called Little Black Pearl (2006)[14] prior to his eventual founding of the Dorchester Project.

The youngest (and the only male) of nine, Gates was influenced by his older sisters, who were a conduit of Black awareness through their affirmative action struggles.[15] Honoring his parents, the artist praises his father's entrepreneurial skills, later visually referencing the senior Theaster Gates's roof repair business by spreading tar—black and thick—on canvases or found objects. He also speaks of his mother's strong religious outlook, saturated in grace. Gates's art strategies also connect to this religious upbringing. His family established a spiritual home at New Cedar Grove Missionary Baptist Church on the West Side. By the early age of thirteen, Gates served as its youth choir director, noting that "my job was to make people feel."[16] This religious history is cited as the source for the philanthropic commitments ensconced in Gates's art-making philosophy. Indeed, Gates asserts that growing up in the Black church taught him that "the pie gets bigger when you give it away."[17] This theological promise and practice of God's abundance further shaped Gates's imagination to view abandoned buildings as things awaiting restoration.[18]

Commuting to school outside of East Garfield Park, Gates gained a wider impression of Chicago's neighborhoods. He noticed how beautiful buildings would fall into disrepair or disappear altogether. This consciousness of locality, how buildings represent homes, people, and neighborliness, would eventually lead to his studies in urban development at Iowa State, where he also discovered ceramics.[19] Both informed his new role as art administrator for Chicago's public transit system, commissioning artists to beautify stations. Gates continued his studies at Iowa State, receiving a graduate degree in urban planning, ceramics, and religion. All these discourses figure later in Gates's urban art endeavors, which also include the soul sounds of his musical ensemble, the Black Monks of Mississippi.

Perhaps because he wears so many hats, Theaster Gates contends that *art* isn't the word he leads with as he reconfigures his South Side Chicago neighborhood of Grand Crossings. Despite this claim, Gates is understood to be a driving force in the currently relevant category of *social practice art*,[20] receiving numerous accolades.[21] This type of art is concerned with social issues and creating social interactions. Calling out systemic failures, artists have planted gardens, installed libraries, and served meals. They have initiated programs for immigrants, the formerly incarcerated, and the unhoused. While projects may appear like social work, as art they encourage repair by employing critique, awareness, and imagination. As in traditional object-oriented art forms, social practice art provides symbolic meaning, which often supplants the object itself.[22] This is exemplified in Jody Wood's *Beauty in Transition*. Wood converted a box truck into a beauty salon to serve residents of New York City homeless shelters. Volunteer estheticians followed the clients' requests as a means to empower and bolster their self-worth. The physical change in each person contains the idea of beauty, but the actual work of art here is how their lives are changed. Rejecting the art-for-art's-sake mantra, social practice art becomes a form of advocacy, creating conduits of social response and responsibility.

Still, Gates is adamant that he is not a "social practitioner" of social practice art works because, in truth, this art-world letter "s" (referring to social settings and systems) is too small.[23] Such classifications only serve to limit. Instead, Gates declares that he leads with belief: "I believe in places, I believe in people, I believe in the value of material things."[24] Creating is an expression of belief, a praxis that addresses the revitalization of neighborhoods, the people in them, and their cultural legacies. This type of belief-through-practice offers Christians a fresh and vigorous model of hospitality.

THE DORCHESTER PROJECT AND A THEOLOGY OF HOSPITALITY

The type of hospitality that is being advocated here is broader than the typical evangelical Christian practice that generates potluck dinners and home Bible studies. Gates is paradigmatic of a wider scope of generosity with what is *other* in the form of place, people, and things. By returning to Grand Crossings, the walk through the Dorchester Project leads to a closer reading of its properties to discern Gates's ethical hospitality.[25] Considering Dorchester Housing + Art Collaborative, Stony Island Arts Bank, and Archive and Listening House will reveal, respectively, Gates's art of staying, where ideas of stewardship are entwined with place, the art of reconciling enterprise, which demonstrates redemption largely in terms of convening diverse elements through labor, and Gates's art of revival, where Spirit enlivens through aesthetic and material means. Indeed, the art of Theaster Gates supplies tangible methods for constructing a theology of hospitality.

Gates's activities provide vistas to glimpse God's inviting character. In other words, the artist's commitment to place enables a thicker comprehension of God's hospitality, inspiring a hallowed regard of physical reality. Gates connects to three specific qualities of divine generosity that provide the framework for a theology of hospitality. The first is the triune God's covenantal concern for creation. The second refers to God's divine and just coherence throughout the cosmos that sustains diversity. And third, the Father and Son through the Spirit uphold the animating function of hospitality as it enlivens place, people, and things. Through art, Gates conveys aspects of God's inviting character via correlating acts of care, reconciliation, and revitalization.

The extensive body of artwork by Theaster Gates presents a platform to critically explore and engage in practices of hospitality. His work also supplies new ways to reanimate Christian traditions through embodied means. Art assists in moving belief from an interiorized relationship with Christ to also participating in social issues as a way to extend God's hosting favor.

Stewardship and the Art of Staying: Dorchester Housing + Art Collaborative

Perhaps defying expectations conferred by his status in the global art world, multi-award-winning artist Theaster Gates has chosen to live in Grand Crossings. Instead of moving to a wealthy neighborhood or a place with hipster cachet, he asks what it would take to be a good neighbor on a rundown street. Taking into account his own artistic need for creative-cultural stimulation, Gates constructs a reciprocal logic of hospitality for the neighborhood. The Dorchester Project creates an atmosphere congenial to artists so they are motivated to stay, and in return, they make the place desirable to others through their cultural and entrepreneurial efforts. By way of this exchange, Gates has found a way to revive the energy lingering still in the deepest roots of the neighborhood.

In order to actually tie artists to Grand Crossings, the organization Rebuild, in collaboration with the Chicago Housing Authority (CHA), Brinshore Development, and Landon Bone Baker architects, took on the task of remodeling an abandoned city-owned housing complex. At the heart of the thirty-two-apartment structure lies an art center established by repurposing four of the units. This conglomeration of living and art space opened in the fall of 2014 as Dorchester Art + Housing Collaborative.

Listed among Dorchester Art + Housing Collaborative amenities, alongside washers and dryers, are art workshops and guided family craft projects. Art is folded into the regular routines of its inhabitants. Through the hands-on ritual of creating together, the art center features a type of hospitality that functions as a conduit for a wide array of physical encounters that makes living deeper and beautiful. Thus, the intimacies of home and hearth combine with art to chip away at the dehumanizing effects of modernity's dissociative stance and the deprivations of the ghetto.

"I may not have the money to restore the entire South Side of Chicago," Gates asserts, "but I do have the capacity to help people re-imagine what the South Side could be."[26] The insertion of art programing within the confines of the housing complex is one such strategy toward cultural and social reimagining. Envision a community that hosts dancers, whose lively pulse reverberates and vivifies tenants and friends to experience and consider a kinesthetic language.[27] What is more, placing an art center in the midst of homes forms in members the habits of hosting. It represents a reimagining of patronage as tenants repeatedly welcome artists, neighbors, and those in the Rebuild network to Dorchester Art + Housing Collaborative.

Beyond establishing housing, the art of staying brings about *home*—appealing places where people can settle—further calling attention to the alienating dislocations of modern living. The art critic Miwon Kwon views site-specific art as both a critical confrontation of contemporary society's loss of place and a corrective. Kwon describes such artistic impulses as "belonging-in-transience,"[28] noting artists' resistance to staying while desiring home. Themes of migration and movement are constitutive of Gates's work, confirming Kwon's diagnosis. Yet his activity of deconstruction-reconstruction serves as a treatment for the malaise of rootlessness. Enlisting an art of staying, Gates introduces a hospitality that is grounded in notions of belonging that are stabilized by the specifics of *place* and the movements therein.

For instance, the art of staying displays for Gates a way to reside locally in order to be "glocal." Despite his international success, Gates lives and produces much of his installation work in Grand Crossings. Additionally, with access to regular exposures to art, the residents of Dorchester Housing + Art Collaborative need not travel outside of Grand Crossings. "What we're telling people is that we want you to stay in this neighborhood and grow with us,"[29] shares Darren Pollard, one of the artists working with Rebuild. Five of the apartment units in

Dorchester Housing + Art Collaborative are slated for artists whose presence would enhance the aesthetic well-being of neighbors and the community. Twelve units lodge CHA clients, and the remaining eleven apartments are reasonably priced rentals hoping to house creatives in the neighborhood. This mixed-income scenario expands the goal of real-estate ventures beyond the market to permit a better quality of life to a wider range of people. Addressing issues of poverty, safety, maintenance, and urban blight rather than accruing financial status certainly adds a layer of substance to John Colapinto's designation of Gates in *The New Yorker* as "the real-estate artist." Creating "places where moments of beauty can happen"[30] not only transforms everyday life for its inhabitants but proposes an aesthetic economy measured by stewarding the fertile creative properties of the local.

By creating homes, Theaster Gates manifests the characteristic of stewardship. This essential building block of a theology of hospitality distinguishes the generative as well as the ethical side of the Greek idea of *kalos,* in which beauty of form also speaks of the civic dimension of community. Thus, concrete portrayals of love of neighbor not only signal justice but are also beautiful.[31] Christ entered time, history, and the particularity of a place to become a neighbor. By settling in Grand Crossings, Gates literally enters into the tribulations of the South Side neighborhood to further flesh out geographies of hope.

Enlivening a geographic imagination is one reason why Gates has garnered attention, as his art embodies hospitality in the form of attractive dwelling and meeting places. Beyond theories and discussions, the world needs alluring images of what ongoing hospitality could look and feel like.[32] Indeed, the art of staying provides such pictures. Through collaboration with several organizations, Gates devised a way to reanimate a city housing block, enable artists to stay, and further promote neighborly interactions through artful undertakings. The next site visit illuminates the economic system that sustains this type of stewardship, while it also highlights the way Gates's work redeems, reconnects, and unifies.

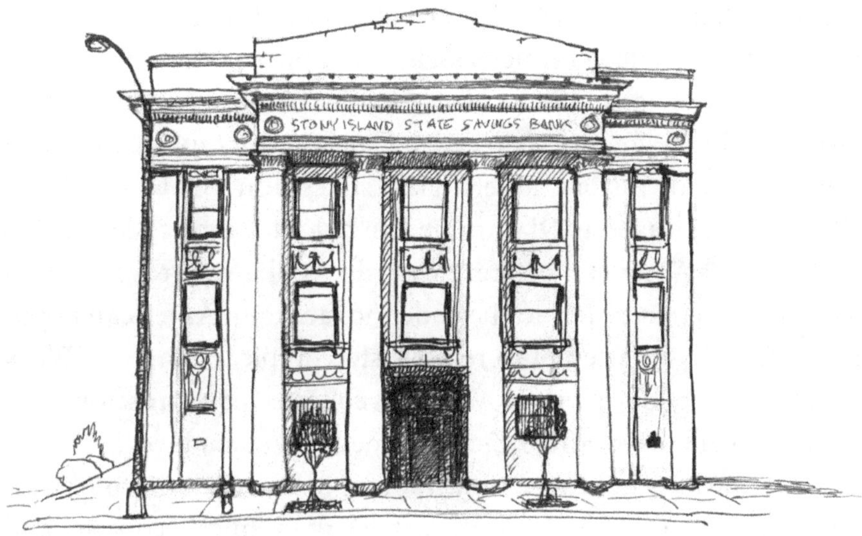

Figure 1.2. Stony Island Arts Bank.

The Art of Reconciliation: Stony Island Arts Bank

Another large-scale renovation cultivated by Gates in Grand Crossings is Stony Island Arts Bank (see figure 1.2). This cultural center evidences the reconciling and restorative quality of a theology of hospitality, which reconnects aspects of God's world that have been ignored or splintered apart. Specific to the Arts Bank is its transformation from abandoned crumbling edifice to active cultural hub. The center displays the art of established Black artists to benefit the local public. It links Black Americans with their historic cultural expressions and further relates this cultural media to the larger fine-art sphere. In these ways, the bank networks a local ecology with global reach as it exhibits Black labor, ingenuity, and fortitude for all the world to see.

The Stony Island Arts Bank opens into a large exhibition hall, where both musical performances and the visual arts are present under surviving portions of its high ornate plaster-cast ceiling. Amiable "gallery coordinators"[33] chat and chill with visitors, shepherding them to a back lounge where they pour cups of fragrant, steaming tea into handmade ceramic vessels. The upper floors hold Gates's collected historical archival materials: John H. Johnson Publishing's research library for the writers for *Ebony* and *Jet* magazines, and some 60,000 art history lantern-glass slides from the University of Chicago. Also saved is DJ Frankie Knuckles's record collection, as well as Black American banker Edward J. Williams's trove of about 3,000 objects that testify to the endemic racism in American popular culture. In an attempt to remove stereotypical images of Black people from antique markets, Williams collected postcards, toys, and household and decorative objects termed *negrobilia* by collectors.

These various holdings, and the method of the building's restoration, aptly communicate the artist's upcycling[34] economy and creative reuse of elements that emphasize Black enterprise. This is a redemptive model that not only signals resurrection through its reuse of Black media or discarded materials but also affirms the inventive and attentive character of Black American wisdom needed to fill the discrepancies resulting from unjust systems.[35] Through such items, Gates leverages a Black history.

Renovations like the bank are established through an alternative funding program wherein Gates repurposes discarded materials to help restore locations. Gates calls his scheme a "circular ecological system"[36] that emphasizes the attributes of the local. The environment offers up an interesting array of materials that include bricks, bowling alley floors, school blackboards, slate shingles, and the contents of a closed hardware store. In addition, the gutted pieces of Gates's own buildings, such as doors, windows, wood planks, and moldings, are also collected and reused to eventually comprise art pieces and installations. Revenue from Gates's sought-after bricolage art constructions enables the purchase and renovation of other properties. This provides more material for more art, and the cycle continues.

The restoration funds for Stony Island Arts Bank offer a perfect example of this intersecting and redemptive ecology that combines art making and place making. After purchasing the condemned bank building from the city for a dollar, Gates raised the required money for renovations by selling marble "bank bonds" engraved with the phrase, "In Art We Trust." Starting at $5,000 for small blocks and up to $50,000 for larger, the bonds were cut from the building's grey-veined marble bathroom stalls, part of the few salvageable materials the deteriorating structure had to offer. With a nod to Duchamp, the bank's urinals entered art world currency. Professor of Arts at Columbia University Carol Becker describes this as alchemy, but Gates calls it joy. It is "the gift of [B]lack folks," he relates, that comes from having to "figure out how to survive." This modifying-through-reconciling-deficiencies impulse is modeled by the way Gates handles objects. He notes that items are not resettled in the absurdist manner of Duchamp's readymades. Instead, a somatic filtration of materials must occur to complete his art process. "It has to come through my body or through my team's body."[37] Through a system that connects land, labor, and materials, cultural goods are validated and presented anew.

The collections held at Stony Island Arts Bank—the Johnson Publishing books and William's artifacts—are also bodily and lovingly filtered through the care, photographing, and cataloging by Rebuild staff and volunteers, illustrating Gates's dictum of Love + Labor = Value.[38] The theorist Edward Soja refers to this type of tactile subject–object interaction as *emplacement* because it tethers beings to place.[39] Through such place making, Gates both deconstructs and reconstructs "social poetics." This is poet Fred Moten's term to describe Gates's aesthetic process that subverts economic enterprise all the while remembering the Black body as commodity.[40] For Gates, the labor of the Black body registers high in this circular ecology. Hence, the Stony Island Arts Bank amplifies the legacy of Black Americans' ingenuity amid daily macro- and micro-aggressions.[41] Through the recirculation of materials and its somatic handling, Gates validates Black labor to employ the art of reconciliation. By devising an enterprise of reuse, he further supports the art of staying to steward the properties of the Dorchester Project. The art of reconciliation, then, works to redeem, reconnect, and unify parts of God's world, ushering life into a neglected neighborhood.

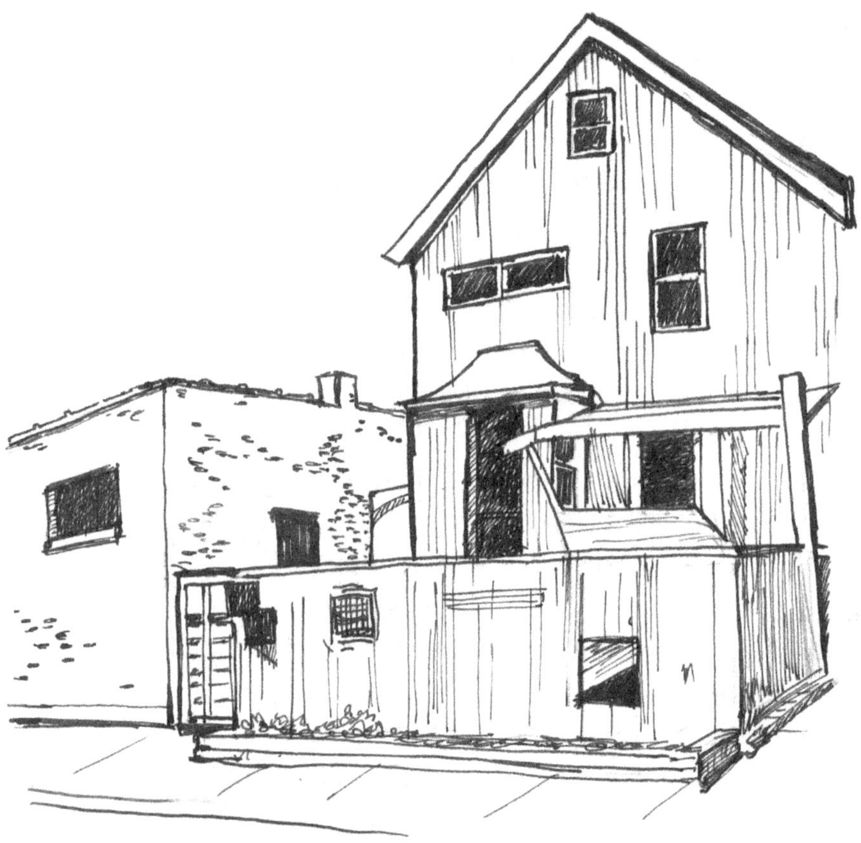

Figure 1.3. Archive House and Listening House.

Art of Revival: Archive House and Listening House

Gates's creative system of capital fuels his restoration habits. His investments are not measured by financial gain but by the increase of life banked in a neighborhood. A visit to the Listening House and Archive House (see figure 1.3) represents this life-giving property under the heading of Gates's art of revival because building restoration points to the feasibility of soul renewal. The impetus to restore is in alliance with God's life-infusing Spirit. For Gates, artistic efforts revitalize physical matter, claiming that "materials and spaces have life in them." Hence, his job as an artist is to bring out the "sacred inside."[42] Through this art of revival, he reanimates abandoned houses, decommissioned fire hoses, and retired collections of books, magazines, and vinyl record albums. A belief in material things allows for items to be saved, and by doing so, Gates affects human souls, signaling redemption of all things. The key term *vitality* can be used to describe "where life meets the spirit"[43] in Gates's work. Gates corrals the spiritual through his ability to notice, re-work, and re-position items.[44] It is an emancipating investment that anticipates dividends of pulsing life.

The Listening House is Gates's earliest purchase. It first served as his home and studio, and eventually housed the rescued stock inventory of Dr. Wax's Record Shop—a chain of neighborhood record stores now no longer in existence. These items were given a new life through their designation as cultural research materials. Admission to the Listening House meant unrestricted access to the rows of shelved albums. And, of course, playing these old records offered participants a different kind of freedom. The very act of placing a soul record on the turntable, and expectantly stationing the needle on a particular track, presents a very specific piece of life to the listener. A funk, samba, or hip-hop playlist can negotiate the felt discrepancies of life by recalling a deeper rhythm to entice the body back into its humanness. What is more, the Listening House supplies a communal version of this soul refreshment through a series of listening parties.

Attached to the Listening House by a wooden trellis and gate is the Archive House. Here Gates initially kept the glass slide library from the University of Chicago's art history department. The DIY construction ethos of the Archive House—both inside and out— utilizes salvaged building materials that engage the imagination and embody Gates's belief in the life found within. Visiting the Archive House is like walking through a living sculpture where mismatched building scraps are delightfully assembled to fashion a zappy sink vanity, a Russian Constructivist stair banister, and a canopy running the length of a passageway. The ability to make much out of little catalyzes creativity and reflects the Christian idea of redemption— receiving the unfit and repositioning it for new life.

Migration's Revival

Gates's upcycle process has an important relationship to the conditions of human migration. This *modus operandi* refers to the postures of adaptability and transposition seen in the greater Black diaspora and the Great Migration of Black Americans from the rural South to the North, Midwest, and West (1916–70). A fitting example of the aggregation, rearrangement, and dispersion of objects is demonstrated in Gates's migration carts—a series of sculptures on wheels. Heaped with household elements, the carts are especially poignant given the current rise of global refugee situations.[45] His amassed items reference their former identity while gaining new traction in different settings, thereby liberating a wide range of capacity and meaning.[46] This negotiation of the poetic is a necessary element of hospitality. By creating places for proximity and the linking of distinct entities, hospitality subsequently becomes a method that unifies.

Through Gates's methods, the artistic customs of the colonized, excluded from the chronicles of Western art history, are now acknowledged. Take, for example, Gates's tall shoeshine thrones made from reclaimed wood, which also bear a visual resemblance to the seating for those leading church services found near the altar. Through these chairs, Gates leverages the labor of the shoeshiner and the preacher, which then alludes to the saving of soles/ souls, and thereby crisscrosses the material and immaterial, an example of "relocation as aesthetic assertion."[47] Such management of materials reveals the life of objects related to the political and the personal—and the multiple meanings in between.[48] This is the redemptive scheme behind Gates's archival gathering and later dispersion of saved objects. These vivifying acts speak of Christ's Spirit, who is not only the giver of life but who also undergirds the renewal of all things. Therefore, Gates's spiriting actions work in anticipation of kingdom renewal where more than souls are saved. The life force that birthed creation into being works to liberate it from its bondage to decay and exploitation. Those who seek the goodness of the created order will answer the Spirit's cry to care for it.

Reviving the Ghetto

Gates's use of a migration method not only revives place, people, and material things but also reveals why hospitality is required. Previously, Miwon Kwon noted that site-specific art carried a critical function that confronts contemporary society's detached attitude toward place.[49] The Dorchester Project not only reflects the migration histories of Black Americans but also reveals the color lines that created ghettos. Neighborhoods like Grand Crossings were formed through race-restrictive covenants between private residents and the Real Estate Board's Code of Ethics.[50] Redlining not only bound Black Americans to live in certain areas but also thwarted career opportunities and social advancements. This was accomplished through aggressive, even violent means. Chicago's ghettos are undeniably fashioned by racism.

The Dorchester Project also brings to light the ways in which location is taken for granted—or understood as something that could be easily stolen, manipulated, commoditized, or used as a source for power and financial gain. As an example of this kind of indifference, consider the frequently offered pulpit refrain that church is about people, not a building. While in a theoretical sense correct, this statement blithely undermines the valuable connections between community, the specificity of place, and how location plays a key role in both individual and collective formation (not to mention the role that sacred space has played in religious practice).

Academic social studies similarly dismiss the significance of geographic attributions. One of the reasons for this disregard is fear of environmental determinism supplanting self-determinism. Paying attention to place promotes territorial adherence that justifies specific cultural characteristics.[51] To be subjected to the contingencies of place calls accountability to it, thus contradicting the idea of human autonomy that floats above the circumstantial. Gates counters this bias as he works to leverage inner-city life—the ghetto—to make it attractive and accessible, a place where people can meet and play, live and grow together.[52] His actions help to develop a spatial imagination that benefits human flourishing by investing in the particularities of place.

ARTISTIC INFLUENCES IN PLACE MAKING

People who practice hospitality have been shaped by the hosting habits of others—they are recipients of grace.[53] For Gates, there are artistic place-making precedents. Rick Lowe's Project Row Houses[54] is the primary model for Gates's art of staying. In 1993 the painter and installation artist Rick Lowe organized artists, art institutions, churches, and other community members to renovate twenty-two row houses in Houston's Third Ward. Lowe and company converted sixteen houses into art-related spaces and dedicated six homes to the purpose of providing single mothers with an opportunity for rent-free living. One of the first residents of the Young Mothers program, Assata Shakur, passionately affirms the venture: "I am really here in graduate school at Penn

State because Rick created Project Row Houses . . . he invested; he saw; he created; he put these ideas into being, and this is the result of his ideas and his creativity. We are his living art forms, which function throughout life."[55] This testimony relays the transformational qualities of art's hospitality.

While Gates's urban renovations reflect the work of artists like Rick Lowe, they also proceed from congregational hospitality. The following theological assessment concerning the Black American church provides some measure of the rationale behind Gates's *poiesis*—his good works that follow the liberating movements of Black American Christianity. Here Gates draws attention to living models of a theology of hospitality. Thereby, he provides the means to credit collective Black struggles, which have paved the way for other disparaged people to seek justice and bestow grace.

A THEOLOGICAL EXPLORATION ON THE HOSPITALITY OF THE BLACK AMERICAN CHURCH

Since Theaster Gates grew up in the Black church, it is not difficult to connect his sociopolitical, poetic, and spiritually infused praxis to the church's home-making propensities. The limiting of opportunities, the "vast veil" strung up by the white world,[56] fashioned an industrious Black Christianity forced to prosper amid restrictions. This liberating power fuels Gates's place-making strategies looking to glimpse God at work in contested places. Gates's work further illuminates a liturgical circular transaction that highlights the power behind corporate church practices as they find their way into localities like Grand Crossings and, consequently, the art world.

Viewed through a framework of a theology of hospitality, Black churches exercised faithful stewardship, faithful liberating and reconciling labors, and faithful spirituality as ways to create home in hostile environments. The following exploration into these three operations not only reveals rich home-making practices but also displays and models a type of belief that interweaves sacred and secular to further God's hospitable commitment to planet Earth. Thus, the Black church embodies a sacramental Protestantism that is liturgically oriented as it offers good works for and by its people, which are further perpetuated on the world's stage by Theaster Gates.[57] Moreover, similar art endeavors by others can cycle back into faith communities to broaden or refresh corporate church practices.

FAITHFUL STEWARDSHIP

If care and maintenance is a quality of a theology of hospitality, then human place making becomes a way to mirror God's covenantal care of his creation. Indeed, a biblical view of the earth's cultivation is closely tied to Yahweh worship. Israel was to play the host of God's bounteous gifts to other nations, understanding that they were always to be guests, aliens dependent on Yahweh's provision.[58] Hence, humanity, made in the image of God, is to reflect God's hospitality by being present to it.[59] Through the reception of grace, Israel was to create bonds of sociability through the land's abundance. Conversely, the mishandling of creation sullies the image-bearing witness of God that further signals a rupture between God and persons. Biblically, when the flow of God's economy of grace is withheld, a divine voice, expressed through the dismay of the prophets, sides against the landed, complicit in issues of poverty and displacement.[60] This prophetic voice is sounded through the works of Theaster Gates, as well as the Black American church.

Black American neighborliness attends to various states of need, exhibiting the stewarding mode of a theology of hospitality in the midst of discrepancies. Indeed, in certain places and times, the Black church functions as a negotiating agent to maintain and nurture the spiritual, educational, economic, cultural, and political dimensions of Black life amid all types of segregation.[61] Systemic racism necessitates creative solutions to energize Christ's liberative power to dispense home-making deeds.[62] Black scholars have credited direct and indirect hostilities as the impetus for innovation, entrepreneurship, and creative improvisation that has become the hallmark of Black cultural ventures.[63] Such ingenuity and survival tactics are evident in Gates's work.

In a reconciling effort to make a way where there was no way, many religious institutions have invested in liberating labors, endeavors that emancipate and illustrate the ways creative genius can be generated by absence or constraints. Church activist John Perkins views this survival skill as stewarding justice. "Justice," he notes, "is our management of God's resources." Perkins's collective approach wonders why some control God's bounty while others are oppressed by selfish accumulation of goods.[64] This corresponds with Gates's concept of leveraging, in which he talks about appreciating a single artist's money-making practice, but then poses a question concerning stewardship: "How do you create bigger platforms that don't just benefit one person, they start to benefit a whole bunch of people?"[65] Faithful custodianship understands wealth in relationship to its impact on others. The joy of home economics is sharing what you have—including the power to nurture people's abilities.

FAITHFUL LIBERATING AND RECONCILING LABORS

It is humbling to encounter models of collective durability in a society that elevates autonomous identity over communal expressions of belonging. Ideas of freedom, creativity, success, and entrepreneurship are turned upside down when viewed through the lens of collective Black resistance. For instance, in the Reconstruction-era, free but segregated Black Americans created religious communities, which also established pathways to financial viability. Scholars Eric Lincoln and Lawrence Mamiya's research regarding the church's role in the rise and fall of Black consciousness discloses the way civil rights–era endeavors reanimated this social-economic legacy; thus, churches readopted entrepreneurship to include business transactions to benefit neighborhoods. Lincoln and Mamiya specifically point to the work of Baptist minister Leon Sullivan, who, in the 1960s, initiated Opportunities Industrialization Centers and the Opportunities Investment Cooperative.[66] The former dealt with community-based job-training efforts to produce employment prospects, while the latter created a mixed for-profit/nonprofit investment cooperative for churches and their members. The investment scheme resulted in the first Black-owned shopping mall, while the nonprofit allotment afforded housing, education, and other social services.

In more recent history, congregations have conducted similar liberating labors. Faith communities have implemented preschool programs and job-training initiatives; they have established business enterprises and educational opportunities, and have also realized financial lending alternatives in order to break the cycle of poverty generated by racial inequalities. Rooted in the sweeping social reach of the early Black church, they model a work and faith integration that steps into the public sphere. Such "partial differentiation"[67] is patterned from a communal view of reality over and against the separations that result from the secular principle of autonomy. Holding this ethos, Black American communities managed God's household provisions to practice the reconciliatory and economic dimensions of hospitality. Gates's circular ecology that sustains the Dorchester Project certainly bears a likeness to the integrative and faithful practices of the Black church.

FAITHFUL SPIRITUALITY

The spiritual is another important characteristic of Theaster Gates's work, which supports interconnectedness yet allows for distinction. It corresponds with an African worldview possessing communal and unifying dimensions, and thus presents a softer approach to Western delineations, especially between sacred and secular. The cohesive outlook of many Black Americans can be described as the "[B]lack sacred cosmos."[68] Within this perspective, all things hold together *and* carry spiritual significance. Perhaps this is why Gates can refer to the Dorchester Project in divine terms, asking, "What if I understood the sacredness of the city and that it is manifested through the things that I make?"[69] While church as a place is vital in rooting, organizing, and shaping collective devotion, Black spirituality is not just restricted to church, its building, or its institutions.[70] A holistic cosmology interconnects the material and immaterial as it supports interrelations. Thus, the spiritual works its way into daily operations, making all kinds of labor sacred.

For Gates, art practice as sacred activity sanctions freedom to migrate across entrenched occupational lines. He states, "I think I am a full-time artist, a full-time urban planner, and a full-time preacher with an aspiration of no longer needing any of those titles."[71] Faithful spirituality attends to what is required, and as a result, encompasses various roles. In the next chapter, Gates is referred to as a monk, an appropriate label when the job description is to manifest the sacred.

Investigating aspects of Black American spirituality reveals the reasons behind Gates's holistic approach. Its root is a comprehensive perspective stemming from an African belief that God links everything through "a circular relationship."[72] Therefore, knowledge, personal growth, or even divine revelation only comes about through interrelationships with place, people, and things. On a social level, this highlights why hospitality is so vital in Black American communities. The unifying activities of hospitality present ways to soften a Western worldview devoted to departmentalization.

What is more, the spiritual proclivity, or supernatural orientation, of Black Americans models ways to administer life amid brokenness, suffering, and oppression.[73] The vivifying dimension of a Black sacred cosmos that aligns with the unifying characteristic of God ultimately upholds relationality. Through liberating labors, Gates and the Black American church present an integrated worldview where activities of restoration are designated as soul works—spiritual endeavors that seek to emancipate creation's full potential. Reformed theologians often refer to such management under the heading of cultural mandate, expressed in terms of human domination over creation. This stance generates a distancing subject–object relation of human supremacy, which perpetuates an instrumental view of creation. Being that the Black American church arose from within a state of oppression—its people seen as mere appliances—it follows a Protestant work ethic[74] that carries the timbre of liberation. The pneumatological initiation of creation as reported in Genesis verifies the Spirit's role in liberating the quiddity of place, people, and things.

By following the wind of God, human activity addresses vast voids—explores long-neglected capacities. There seems to be an emancipatory transaction of the Spirit in respect to reconciliation, especially in terms of the "human struggle" to dignify those "in an inhuman situation." Through God's presence via the Spirit, a work and faith integration ensue when the "blood, sweat, and tears" of a suffering community become the means toward change.[75] In this way, labor, both Christ's and his followers', constitute redemptive acts. Reconciliation is then a "*project* of freedom" that looks to realize the "divine right of creation."[76] Rather than commence ventures from a stance of dominion, culture care arises from hospitality; the desire to benefit place, people, and things.

A LITURGICAL ETHOS: CONCLUSION

The liturgies of the Black church are methods that maintain God's abode. They offer unifying practices and designate human labors as spiritual. Influenced by the church, Gates's social–political–spiritual brand of art is to be understood as liturgical. The enterprises of both Gates and faith communities bear some resemblance to certain patronage liturgies of the medieval church. During this period, guilds and craftsmen would sponsor liturgical celebrations that would fund care for the sick. Thus, hospitality is historically linked to Christian liturgical operations of repair that are the foundation for modern-day hospitals.

Indeed, the liturgical order is based on God's love and commitment, therefore it presents an alternative social program that urges people to depend on one another. This differs from public interactions set by the dispassionate tone of the Enlightenment's rationalism.[77] The liturgical provides an empathic means to *enter* into the lives of others. The Dorchester Project displays a commitment of welcome. Gates's stewardship of place, a practice honored in the art world, provides a liturgy of the urban landscape that is fashioned by the heavy marks of labor borne by the Black church for the sake of community.

By visiting the Dorchester Project, people are asked to consider the sacredness of place and the ways God's hospitality is manifested through human labor. Gates's work further challenges Christian ideas of neighborliness while concurrently inspiring all to convert distressed city streets into poetic places.

2

Hospitality and People: *To Speculate Darkly*

"There's a way in which artists might have the power to conjure
the symbolic, to do things in the world that other folks couldn't
imagine."

—Theaster Gates[1]

In 2010, the Milwaukee Art Museum displayed a visual conversation
between two potters: Dave Drake, an enslaved potter from antebellum South Carolina, and contemporary artist Theaster Gates. The
show's title, *To Speculate Darkly,* is Gates's invitation to perform
reflective action by considering slavery and post-slavery Black American life and production. The exhibition further presents the ways
Gates's work aligns with the three distinctive qualities of a theology of
hospitality—care, reconciliation, and vivification. To be sure, *To
Speculate Darkly* stewards and reconciles the underrepresented cultural expressions of people of color. And, in order to be a light in
the dark, Gates encourages one cultural institution to host multiple
embodied art forms as liberating social signifiers, subsequently fashioning a hospitable public place to restore all people.

Through his experiences as a potter and performer, Gates curates
welcoming spaces where art affirms the worth of brown and Black
bodies. In *To Speculate Darkly,* Dave Drake becomes the honored

guest, and the impetus for Gates to once more tackle the theme of Black labor. One of the particular aims of the exhibition is to show the worth of overlooked workers, which then authenticates all persons through tangible art experiences. Concerning the first intent, Drake symbolizes and epitomizes Black American slave labor, an icon of human subjugation, a mere apparatus for white economic opportunity embroiled in unjust social systems. Yet, as an artist, the enslaved potter also represents resistance mediated through creative ingenuity. Drake exemplifies a rare instance in early Black American craft where actual attribution is present. Having established a legacy of signed vessels, Drake's literacy as a slave signals rebellion against imposed limitations. The pots bear his name and are also adorned with curious, poetic couplets such as "I saw a leppard, & a lions face / then I felt the need of—Grace."[2] By way of focused handwork, clay becomes the host for an enslaved voice, a way to endure hardships.

Through collaborations, artistic objects, and gestures that accompany Drake's work at the Milwaukee Art Museum, Gates amplifies the potter-poet's inscribed utterances as a means to honor all unnamed enslaved potters, as well as the many invisible laborers that have fed the cultural pulse of nations. This chapter displays art's hospitality through the poetics of performance, making the body in motion a tangible and felt route to express belief in all people. In Milwaukee, art becomes the vehicle whereby God's hospitality extends outside of the church to the museum, by way of Gates's speculation.

HOSPITABLE PERFORMANCE: *TO SPECULATE DARKLY*

Dave Drake's large storage jar is the centerpiece of *To Speculate Darkly*, the raison d'être for Gates's surrounding multimedia art schemes. The utilitarian vessel receives a place of honor to visually correspond with Western treasures like the Greek vases lining the halls of the Metropolitan Museum of Art. Dramatically illuminated, the jar assumes a religious aura that demands hushed reverence from visitors. To reach the relic, one has to traverse a darkened anteroom with a ceiling lit using art-history glass slides picturing Roman, Greek, and Eastern cultural objects, yet devoid of any African articles. Gates again alludes to this cultural lapse in the next gallery by way of a large wall-size relief insignia for the Association of Named Negro American Potters (ANNAP). This plaster-like medallion is a chimerical device since the organization, of which Gates deems himself president, is one that has never existed. Also, to be found in the main gallery is a wall quote on the nature of lower-class workers sinking below their own marginality, while another text signals the inclusion Gates is after:

> *For all of the named potters in the world*
> *And all of the named Negro heroes*
> *I'd like to add myself to your canons*
> *My name goes here.*

Thus, the exhibition begins with negation—a black hole that Gates aims to fill. The ambition of *To Speculate Darkly* is to inscribe and ascribe names. It is the medium for Gates's hospitality to welcome muted voices. In another gallery, the volume gets literally turned up as we view faces on video monitors intoning moans of gospel-sounding lament. Music also emanates from a wall installation featuring a grid of shallow modern ceramic sinks. Gates formulated these wares with the help of the Chipstone Foundation as the artist-in-residence at Kohler Company in Milwaukee.[3] The commercial sinks playfully become the modern equivalent to Drake's large clay pots. Both are commodities forged through Black ingenuity, and it is poignant to note that the music that streams from the clay speakers is composed from the poetic couplets inscribed on Dave Drake's pots. Thus, ceramic goods—from the hands of an enslaved potter and Kohler's manufacturing process—converge to become audio conduits that transmit the yearning for designation.

To create the sound performance elements of *To Speculate Darkly*, Gates donned his old choir director hat from his days at Cedar Grove Missionary Baptist Church to assemble and supervise a chorus comprised from neighboring Milwaukee Black churches and Chicago artists. Together, they intoned and recorded Drake's poetic stanzas.[4] In addition, Gates visually recognized the choristers by stenciling their names onto one of the gallery walls. He further arranged for the institution to grant them a free membership. In this way, Gates inserted an underrepresented people group into the museum context as both artists and patrons. For the live gospel performance event of Drakes's stanzas, the eighty-person recorded choir swelled to two hundred. Parading through the museum with resonant presence, this choral convocation inverted the typical white art museum into a Black monumental place.

THE THEOLOGY OF SPECULATING DARKLY

Through artistic gestures, Gates's stewarding impulse validates and cares for underrepresented persons. His insertion of Black production into a predominately white-occupied space reconciles, in part, more diverse expressions of God's creation. The exhibition further emphasizes the aesthetic dimension of Gates's spirituality, where Black bodies in poetic motion assist in amplifying the Spirit in the secular realm. In these ways, Gates's performances host divine–human connections for all.

The subject of inclusion leads to an understanding of Gates's work in terms of ratifying the theological doctrine of *imago Dei*. The artist's belief in people aligns with the notion that all are made in the image of God; hence all of humanity holds the capacity to reflect God's hospitality. Gates's art methods *conjoin* religious expressions with art forms to bring forth emancipatory movements for all people, especially for persons of color.

The act of *conjoining* aligns with Hispanic/Latinx theology. The term *en conjunto* denotes a theological method that links life's embodied and collective experiences to abstract theological assessments as a way to empower marginalized persons made in the image of God. Theologians Anthony Pinn and Benjamin Valentin describe later liberation theologians' efforts as the "struggle for subjectivity."[5] In many ways, Gates's art performs in continuity with the work of second-generation liberation theologians desiring to claim personhood for the underrepresented. Theological activity conjoined with communal images, narratives, and gestures is a method that brings about the social transformation of individuals, ethnic communities, and society at large. *En conjunto* theology regards quotidian and cultural expressions as the means of decolonization, which broadens theology by providing distinctive perspectives.[6] In a similar way, Gates's creative efforts—his gathering and repositioning of items, materials, and people—grant new possibilities. Since art transmits life's meaning in a visceral way, it allows people "to conjure the symbolic, to do things in the world that other folks couldn't imagine."[7] In the mode of liberation theology, Gates models a way for artists to spiritually uplift others.

Stewardship of Black Bodies

Conjoining art with theological performances of liberation is paramount in present history amid the worldwide refugee crisis, the spectacle of a US border wall, the Black Lives Matter movement, and systemic racism within law enforcement. Addressing hospitality's qualities of care, reconciliation, and revival as seen through Gates's handling of the black hole of Black American production becomes the means for the viewer to reinvest in Christian hospitality. *To Speculate Darkly* affirms and amplifies the way art is a valuable enterprise that enables acceptance and care of what is other.

Through Gates's belief in people, he *conjures* ways to care for persons by establishing arenas where art experiences—both making and viewing—lead to personal and communal transformation. Evaluating Gates's work, there are three specific ways he stewards the worth of persons. First, the poetic permits possession and validation of self. Second, art builds resilience and navigates acts of resistance. And third, art's hospitality formulates a type of visible and tangible public presence—a monumental place—that must be acknowledged.

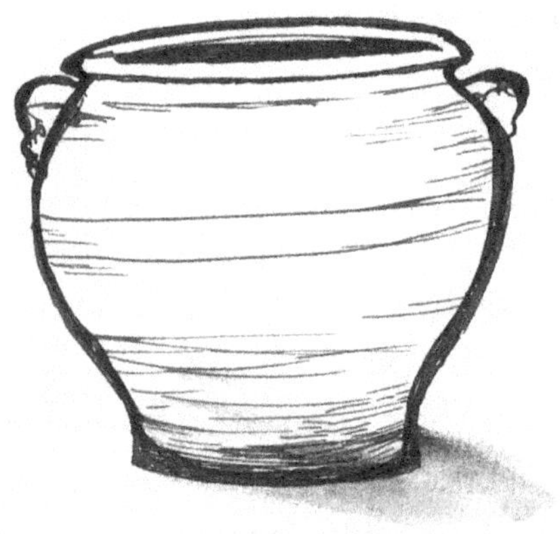

Possession of Self

Art experiences enable the construction of participants' subjectivity or selfhood. Self-possession occurs as this experience supplies care for souls while their worth becomes materialized. Gates's art collaborations invite Black artists into these ameliorative processes. To understand the operations behind such experiences, theologian Karl Rahner outlines the continuum between embodied self and poetic output. Working on the premise that all persons naturally rely on the symbolic,[8] Rahner asserts that in order to know the self, one expresses aspects of the self through symbolic means. Accordingly, such realization produces a "plurality in unity."[9] For instance, there is the potter Dave Drake, and then there are multiple expressions of Drake formulated through his many versed pots. As Rahner puts it, "one reality renders another present" and "allows the other to be there."[10] In other words, art production confirms the maker's being-ness as it outwardly projects vital items that in turn symbolize and materialize their personhood. Artistic representation is especially valuable when it comes to marginalized persons since it provides tangible proof that they exist. An example of this operation from *To Speculate Darkly* is video footage of vocalists channeling Dave Drake by singing his couplets. This provides a place for the vocalists to house and project their own pain in a meaningful and healing way.

Sounding out both Drake's and their own longings, performers invite museum visitors to enter into lament. This charged poetic place hosts an emotional exchange between artist and guest. Through empathetic means, Gates provides the avenue for double subjectivity that subverts Black double-consciousness.[11] Singers are given room to attend to self through their musical performances, and subse-quently they become the subject through which visitors receive poetic cries of Blackness. Viewing this occurrence through Rahner's logic, there is a direct connection between *beingness* and its substantive manifestations. Whether through cryptic couplets or melodious wailings, art provides the place for the "possibility of possession of self."[12] *To Speculate Darkly* is the platform that leads its performers to self-possession, an affirmation of personhood.

Resilience and Resistance

As struggle and Black labor is integral to Gates's work, he further emphasizes art's ability to mediate human survival. For example, while Dave Drake fashioned pots intended for ordinary household use, the ceramic pieces also operate as symbolic extensions of self-declared dignity that relieves despair. Gates's creation of the fic-tional ANNAP relief insignia in *To Speculate Darkly* operates in the same manner. These symbols of yearning for designation produce resilience through art-making transactions. When living is restricted, the creative process provides alternate renditions of what can be; it furnishes ways *to do things in the world.* Thus, *making* manufactures remedy or hope in small measure. Simultaneously, it enables an elastic knowledge where discoveries, mishaps, the manipulation of materials become the basis for innovation, increased wisdom, and perseverance. Art making holds a type of bodied intelligence that informs the handling of other life situations. Such crafting reveals how much can be made of little, which further produces ingenious survival[13] methods that seek to restore. In this way, Dave Drake's poetic couplets render an ethos of endurance through the activity of tactile clay production.

Because the Black body is a "prototype of abjection," industry is one pathway to realize and sustain self-confidence. This is another reason why labor is such an important topic in Gates's oeuvre. The Black body in motion represents resistance, as it provides the means for new forms of Blackness to rise up and replace the stigmatized body.[14] Seen in this light, Drake's poetic voice written on pottery overturns a limited imagination that assumes the improbable literacy of the enslaved. Gates's inscription of collaborators' names on a gallery wall (alongside their museum membership) also looks to resist the debilitating discrepancies of rejection. Art counters the sting of exclusion as it simultaneously builds muscles of resilience.

Monumental Place

Art's liberating actions establish presence. Art is a concrete, visible, felt, or audible articulation that others must negotiate within the confines of time and place. Besides a route to self-discovery, the symbolic is described by Rahner as "the reality in which *another* attains knowledge of a being." Performance, then, becomes the way to project a person's "invisible figure outside itself" through the symbolic.[15] Ceramic pots, poems, liturgies, and laments assert the solidity of presence for others to acknowledge. What is more, art houses and projects a set of symbols stemming from the sociopolitical–religious reality of its creators. The combining of these symbols forms a specific kind of property, a monumental place that others can either join or reject.[16]

A perfect example of this corporeal ratification is when Gates inserts an ambulatory Black gospel choir throughout the halls of the Milwaukee Arts Museum to perform Dave Drake's couplets. It is what choreographer Ronald K. Brown terms a transformational parade movement that displays a portrait of "people going somewhere." Brown and Black bodies in motion signal a progressive power to conjure a moving public entity.[17] Gates's hospitality entails the forward-moving direction of art that empowers, builds tenacity, and constructs a tangible presence that confronts. He not only nourishes the souls of artists; he also invites museum guests to consider their gifts.

THE BLACK HOLE: RECONCILING DISPARITY

Theaster Gates is not only preoccupied with the way art employs the whole person but also with how it should engage all people. Within the framework of a theology of hospitality, Gates looks to reconcile the productive activity of people of color within predominantly white art spaces. Since the 1990s, inclusivity has been touted in the postmodern rhetoric of the art world, asserting how former minor players deserve a level playing field. Yet a black hole has continued to exist in the art world pertaining to brown and Black representation.[18] Of late, this landscape has begun to shift with the increasingly positive work of the Black Lives Matter movement and its response to the high-profile police killings of Black Americans.[19] For instance, *ArtReview*'s Power 100, a feature that yearly takes stock of the most influential people in the art world, had included six Black and six Latinx people in its 2017 list. By 2019, the numbers doubled.[20] "If the art world can accept being 'about Iceland,'" Gates had noted in 2011, "Why can't we be about a Black church storefront on the South Side of Chicago?" Gates maintained that gaps exist "in the contemporary art world that nobody can fill except really specific people."[21] This reality prompted Gates to feature the crew of singing storefront church people through the halls of the Milwaukee Art Museum. Through the efforts of others like Gates, the black hole is slowly being filled.

Trickster

One way Gates addresses the kind of art-world inequalities that he has personally experienced is through creative subterfuge. Regarding the strategy behind the storefront church choir parade, Gates challenged Milwaukee Museum staff regarding lack of Black patronage. With a tone of incredulity and a touch of scorn, he contends, "You just gotta invite people."[22] By assembling the large gospel choir for *To Speculate Darkly*, invitations were extended to local church vocalists, thus creating an impetus for their faith communities, family members, and friends to visit the museum. Speaking generally of his work, Gates claims that he is somewhat of a trickster, explaining, "I want to seduce you with an object, and I don't even want you to know of my social agenda. The object will be a key. As the result of the seduction, you find yourself concerned with questions of places and people."[23] Adopting the Black American trickster motif in the vein of Brer Rabbit, the spider Anansi, and the role reversals and ruses of early Black theater, Gates activates the *resistance* mode of art meant to ward off alienation and limitations.[24] The trickster transforms the harsh realities of Black life by turning things inside out in order to conjure Black legitimacy—*to do things in the world that other folks couldn't imagine.*

A Performance of Absence: My Life as a Dog

One art historical antecedent to Gates's trickster tactic was played out by the artist Fred Wilson in 1992. Wilson performed *My Life as a Dog* to import Blackness into the premier art venue of the Whitney Museum. To commence the performance, the artist gathered museum docents in the lobby and instructed them to meet him on an upper floor. Wilson quickly changed into a security guard uniform and stood in the arranged meeting spot. Unable to *see* Wilson because of the uniform, the docents wandered throughout the galleries in search of him.[25]

Wilson's performance relates the facelessness of being Black, and the way Black persons are typically expected in the museum to be lowly security guards.[26] Thus, Wilson's body in *My Life as a Dog* penetrates a specific narrative in a particular public place, further illuminating an American consensus on Blackness. Wilson's body became a place of negotiation that exposed negation.[27] Similarly, *To Speculate Darkly* began with rooms representing exclusion, but Gates progressively reconciled the Black body through multiple acts of inclusion, finally ending the exhibition with the wall of inscribed names of artist collaborators. For Gates there is beauty in the Black body, which is the site of Black power—the locus of resilience amid the severities of dislocation. At times, Gates addresses this super-power as spiritual power.[28]

SPIRITING PERFORMANCE

Within Gates's Black aesthetic, resistance and resilience are gained through the antics of a trickster, while revival of the soul is rendered through the spiritual.[29] The two qualities are combined when Theaster Gates dons the persona of a monk—especially when he performs with his musical ensemble the Black Monks of Mississippi.

Within the framework of a theology of hospitality, Gates's monkhood pumps life-giving energy into situations. Gates's own spiritual revival experiences, whether church-related or arising from art making, have informed him in such a way that he is able to expose modernism's racism that negates the supernatural. By leaning on Black spiritual power, Gates counters what he perceives as a "cultural hierarchy" based on Western art philosophical processes that snub the ritualistic, the spiritual, or any shamanistic tendencies unless they are performed in ironic fashion.[30] Through a lexicon of Black spirituality, Gates imposes poetic paradigms into the art world that he believes are more fluid, genuine, and transcendent. Consequently, Gates's Black aesthetic provides vivifying moments that he characterizes as spiritual.[31] His Black power performances enable emotional human communion that are normally missing within the high art realm.

The Black Monastic

Besides the gospel soundings of Drake's couplets in *To Speculate Darkly*, the type of spiriting just related is best exemplified in Gates's 2014 performance entitled *Black Monastic*. Here, Gates conceived a ten-day monastic retreat at the Serralves Museum in Porto, Portugal. Gates and the Black Monks of Mississippi set out to listen to one another and respond to the museum's art collection and surrounding grounds through monk-like ritualistic activities. The performances were especially pertinent considering how Portugal's historical colonialism sanctioned slavery as a Christian method to save souls.[32] Thus the ersatz monks' liberating labors altered visitors' perceptions of the museum's Euro-white holdings and their provenance through Black power presence that poetically affected souls.

Is Gates simultaneously a trickster and a spiritual leader? In an interview, he subversively asked, "What if I were to say that I've underplayed the fact that I'm actually a Benedictine monk and . . . that this work that I've been doing, that we've all called art, was just a by-product of a mandate from on high?"[33] What Gates is suggesting here is that it may take the conjoining of the artistic and spiritual to liberate the souls of brown and Black bodies from oppressive regimes. *To Speculate Darkly* illuminates a Black aesthetic by which the body is a monumental place where spirituality unravels the biases of modernity that deny soul work. While the trickster trope may seem duplicitous to some, it works as a way to relate truth through subversive means, establish resistance, and further propose outrageous possibilities to counter injustice. Gates fills the black hole in the white art cube by way of the reconciliatory aim of hospitality, which is grounded by a unified worldview that values inclusivity. What is more, through monkhood, Gates hosts an ameliorative process that feeds hungering souls. This type of performance is based on a relational ethos, a Black sacred cosmos where persons grasp knowledge of self, God, and others through shared activities.

THEOLOGY'S HOSPITABLE PERFORMANCE: *IMAGO DEI—MISSIO DEI*

Gates's poetic expressions that make up *To Speculate Darkly* are people-affirming gestures that embody the theological doctrine of *imago Dei*. One of the first assertions made in Genesis is humanity's iconic status to the divine—we are made in the image and likeness of God (Genesis 1:27). *Imago Dei* confirms brown and Black selfhood that is further validated by the likely dark skin tone of Jesus himself. Tethered to the doctrine are the concepts of icon and idol as well as *missio Dei*, or mission of God actions, all of which are important concerning the visible issues concerning race.

In reference to the qualities of care, reconciliation, and vivification that flow from a theology of hospitality, *missio Dei* reflects and represents God's welcoming hospitality. Indeed, hospitality is the antidote for the denial of *imago Dei* made evident in the idolatrous veneration of whiteness practiced throughout the Western world. Thus, Gates's *missio Dei* labors are needed to restore *imago Dei* status to those deemed inferior. As Gates's monk persona displays, *missio Dei* performances resacralize persons within a prevailing immanent worldview to acknowledge the *more* of being human. Observing Gates's hospitality leads to a theological study that sketches out an *imago Dei* to *missio Dei* framework.[34] This in turn looks to rouse Christian acts of hospitality, liberating projects that expose a belief in all people.

Imago Dei

What constitutes *imago Dei*? How are humans made in the *selem* (image) and *demuth* (likeness) of their creator? Israel, unlike surrounding nations, held a divergent concept of the divine. Most ancient Near East cosmologies viewed the created world as an emanation of a deity. Subsequently, the Hebrew notion of idolatry, the worship of created things instead of the Creator, is based on the pagan belief that the divine is co-mingled with the material; thus, the deity is conjured through the shaping of an idol from earthly matter. Israel countered this pantheism by separating their living God from the physical world.[35] Thus, in the Judeo-Christian tradition, God stands distinct from yet in relation to creation by way of *imago Dei.*

While there are many traditional interpretations concerning the doctrine of *imago Dei*,[36] theologian Richard Lints offers a way of understanding the link between humanity and the divine in terms of *reflection.* As with a mirror, *imago Dei* signifies the way humanity relates to God as the main source for its significance. Like the limitations of a mirror, humans can only reflect God. They are not God.[37] Accordingly, *imago Dei* presents conceptual portraits of the divine to confer meaning. It provides proximity to the divine that helps make sense of human nature and its physicality, faculties, and emotions. Yet, these elements alone do not demonstrate *imago Dei*. It is humanity's *relationship* to God that formulates human identity and mission.[38] In short, for Lints, *imago Dei* is a theological approach that is dependent on the paradigmatic. God is the primary model that fashions human subjectivity and activity.

Icon: Stewardship as Representation

This reflective approach coincides with the royal representative notion of *imago Dei* in which human acts of stewardship mediate and display the divine ethos of God's hospitality. This model is based on the notion of proxy—or icon—whereby a king's power is indicated by a visible stand-in. A coin stamped with a royal's image is one example from the ancient Near East. Another is the placement of a portrait statue of the king indicating his propriety over a terrain. The liturgical language surrounding *imago Dei* in Genesis also bears affinities to ancient Near East rituals that denote kinship lineage, the relationship between a god and progeny.[39] As God's royal offspring, Israel was to portray a desirable image of God to surrounding nations. The intimate status of royal descendant—knowing the hospitable character of God—would bring about proper stewarding or hosting enterprises in order to maintain God's creation.

Unfortunately, many Christians have not borne out this image-bearing feature of God's hospitality. For this reason, Gates steps into the darkness to encourage Black American artists to "do things in the absence of light," passionately adding, "and be Black about it."[40] Theaster Gates provides the mirroring actions Lints speaks of by displaying aspects of a hospitable God in the midst of disheartening traumas executed against Black persons. And in doing so, Gates also sheds light upon the ways Christians have forgotten or denied the doctrine of *imago Dei*.

Idolatry: Denial of *Imago Dei*

When it comes to the subject of race, Christians have rebuffed the concept of *imago Dei*. God's hospitality has been constrained by an idolatrous veneration of the ideal human, usually depicted as a white, rational male. Western programs and social systems, including Christianity, are derived from and uphold philosophical principles that have painted a portrait of Black inconsequentiality to reify white subjectivity. Whether it was the construction of Hegel's *über* human-nation or Jefferson's cupidity that required slave labor, rational arguments denied the universality of *imago Dei* by casting shades of subhumanity onto Black bodies in order to further the progress of Westernization.[41] From religion to science to politics, powerful, "enlightened" men questioned the intellectual and moral capabilities of non-Westerners in order to colonize them. Their corrupt logic sanctioned the purloining of lands, obliterated cultural wisdoms, and demonized the integrated religious worldview of those they enslaved.

Theologian Willie James Jennings highlights the ways the West secured an "iconic position," which formalized particular tastes to comprise an "aesthetic regime"[42] that images and sells a version of the good life.[43] This controlling posture obliges the world to "discern the true, the good, and the beautiful" around the activities of white bodies.[44] For instance, early missionary efforts imposed white iconic standards rather than discover Christ's grace in the narratives, social structures, and beliefs of native peoples. The inability to perform reciprocal or mutual exchange leads Jennings to contend that Christianity holds a "diseased social imagination"[45] as it displays patterns of domination. Both in past and present, Western Christianity regulates what is orthodox, decrees unjust laws, sanctions slavery, determines racial categories, and refutes unfamiliar standards of beauty, as it globally exports their notion of human progress through educational efforts. If *imago Dei* rouses *missio Dei* works, Christianity's mission has been corrupted by imperialistic habits of control that are still at play.

The continual police shootings and the mass incarcerations of Black American and Latinx people, voter suppression laws, the border wall construction, and the nation's immigration policies all point to American Christianity's erasure of *imago Dei*. Instead of displaying the diversity of God's creation, churches place their trust in a religious-political rhetoric steeped in white supremacy. Certainly, such idolatry undermines the Christian mission to care for God's creation. Instead, it takes secular movements like Black Lives Matter to fill the black hole of Christian hospitality.[46] Speculating on this darkness, theologian Luis Pedraja wisely points to a reverse trajectory of iconic human–divine correlation. He notes that if sin is the inability to view God correctly, the consequence is failure to recognize the *imago Dei* in others. Human constructions of race and its disabling results white-out humanity's shared status as God's beloved creatures.[47] What is needed is a Christian practice of hospitality that offers light amid the darkness of a Christian imagination.

ICONIC LOGIC: RECONCILING *IMAGO DEI*

Both an idol and an icon mirror aspects of their maker. An idol displays inordinate desires of the human heart,[48] while an icon expresses *imago Dei*. An idol, then, directs attention away from God. For example, Jennings notes that when whiteness becomes the preeminent reflection of Christianity, all other bodies struggle to conform with or fight against this form of idolatry that diminishes God's manifold witness.[49] On the other hand, hospitality as seen through the art of Theaster Gates presents an iconic reflection of God's hospitality.

Art can assist in the reestablishment of the human–divine link forged by *imago Dei*, thereby reaffirming all people, especially those deemed lesser. The eighth-century Syrian monk John of Damascus believed in art's power to negotiate *imago Dei*. Correlative to the notion of royal image bearer, John of Damascus contends that veneration of an icon—usually a depiction of Christ or one of his servants—is the act of paying respect to God. In his defense of icons, John of Damascus additionally emphasizes an analogous interplay between God and humanity that leads to human worth: "We venerate one another as having a portion of God and having come to be in the image of God, humbling ourselves before one another and fulfilling the law of love."[50] Here the performance of venerating depicted human figures is tied to their worth in God; and this focus ultimately conducts the heart back to God. Hence, icons help people to esteem God's human image bearers. John of Damascus makes clear that people are not gods by their own nature "but as partakers of God's nature, so they are to be venerable."[51] Thus the theologian realigns human worth in relation to God, through an art form. This sheds theological light upon Gates's attention to Dave Drake. *To Speculate Darkly* celebrates the creations of the enslaved potter, someone made in God's image. But Gates also establishes Dave Drake as an icon that represents and affirms undervalued artists and patrons, claiming that "big art does not leave others out."[52] Through a belief in people, Gates and John of Damascus present the ways art mediates *imago Dei*.

Art's capability to honor others is the reason why Jennings revisits Damascus's teaching as a way to prevail against the white aesthetic regime.[53] By advocating new artistic creations, Jennings challenges white supremacy's limited scope of what constitutes *imago Dei*. He argues that the arts can play an appropriate and invigorating role in Christianity, and beyond, by hosting "spaces of the iconic."[54] For this reason, Jennings calls churches to invest in an "*artistic* ecclesiology"[55] that would liberate the creativity of God's people made in God's image. Fashioning new portraits and performances would broaden the faith vocabulary of Christians to rightly represent God's pluriform witness. This iconic logic further counters the negative effects of white idolatry as it performs the poetics of hospitality. As seen in Gates's Dorchester Project, and the iconic space of *To Speculate Darkly,* art hosts transformational and generative possibilities.

SPIRIT SUMMATION: RESACRALIZE

Just as Gates leverages the worth and the work of Black bodies, *imago Dei* negotiates their reification by nudging them toward their fullest potential: divine life with God. Jennings's artistic ecclesiology is one way to realize this concept as a means to disrupt white hegemony. Theologian Miroslav Volf is also wary of the misdirected loyalties surrounding ethnicity. In an attempt to engender loyalty to God rather than to ethnic allegiances, Volf advocates the adoption of a "catholic personality," citing life in Christ as a unifying principle. His aim is to "de-sacralize" ethnicity in order to loosen the claims of kin and nation that drive oppressive behaviors.[56]

While Volf's impetus may be correct, the notion of desacralizing race and ethnicity as a way to reorder human desire unwittingly removes the potential of such platforms from serving as the locus in which God can be found. The prior explorations into the history of Black American life by way of Gates's art reveals how community shapes persons. Therefore, the possibility of addressing God outside of social–cultural structures as Volf advocates are slim.[57] A theology of hospitality confirms that Christian belief is more than an internal process. Matters of race and ethnic identity need not always divert human devotion from God. Lints contends that as image bearers, persons set a "double-refraction" that points both to God and the social–cultural specifics of God's creation.[58] Indeed, Jesus entered the world and wore the cultural features of a place. His messianic supremacy redeems people into the image of a cruciform life that reconciles all things to God.[59] *Imago Dei* resacralizes bodies, cultures, and ethnicities as part of divine hospitality.

Instead of imposing an inward spiritual attitude as Volf suggests, Jennings, with the help of John of Damascus, advocates approaching aspects of the external world like creation, art, and culture with an iconic belief that they are all "meant for communion with God."[60] Theaster Gates in his role as a monk both embodies and is paradigmatic of this movement. The artist provides iconic spaces that mediate what Lints calls the theophanic.[61] Through the Spirit, the divine is made present.

To *Speculate Darkly* presents the body in motion as an inner advocate for the soul and an outer witness to the world. Its creative strategies reflect God's commitment to people, especially those that have been marginalized through white idolatry. Gates's dynamic belief in people points to the theological notion of *imago Dei*, which ratifies and activates human distinctiveness that further leads to enactments of *missio Dei* labors.[62] Mission of God acts are concrete ways in which God's hospitality is dispersed through human labors that care for, reconcile, and revive the earth and everything in it.

"There's a way in which artists might have the power to conjure the symbolic, to do the things in the world that other folks couldn't imagine."[63]

3

Hospitality and Material Things:
Soul Food Pavilion

"I think it is partly about the gathering of people and partly about my ability to put a very specific finger on a certain kind of cultural activity so that just when one thinks they have soul food figured out, it actually reveals itself in all these other ways that have nothing to do with eating."

—Theaster Gates[1]

The Dorchester Project and *To Speculate Darkly* represent the ways in which Theaster Gates both models and embodies the triune God's hospitality. These artworks reviewed in the preceding chapters depict the *imago Dei* to *missio Dei* qualities of stewardship, reconciliation, and spiriting revitalization that comprise the framework of a theology of hospitality. Having tackled Gates's belief in place and people, attention is now drawn to the worth of concrete reality, specifically the phenomena that sustain table fellowship. As the essence of home making, the table represents the beating heart of a theology of hospitality as it necessitates thus certifies place, people, and material things. The tangible items that surround Gates's meal rituals become the locus from which the artist reveals other activities and concerns besides eating.

Soul Food Pavilion is a performance, installation, and object-oriented artwork that contains a series of meal gatherings in Gates's neighborhood of Greater Grand Crossings. The dinners are a part of Smart Museum of Art, University of Chicago's 2012 programming and subsequent exhibition entitled *Feast: Radical Hospitality and Contemporary Art.*[2]

Surveying the dinner performances cracks open the socio-ethical dimensions of the Lord's Supper. Hence, Gates's table points to Christ's table. This assertion is made with a circular liturgical transaction in mind: the power of church meal practices is exerted on Dorchester Avenue through *Soul Food Pavilion.* The circle is completed when Gates's hosting rouses similar Christian reinvestment in ethical meal sharing. In line with a theology of hospitality, both Christ and Gates's tables exhibit stewardship and care, unifying patterns of reconciliation, and a spiritual dimension that deepens the value of place, people, and material things. Moreover, both meals bring to light the way physical things arbitrate symbolic and real effects that enable human communion with God and others.

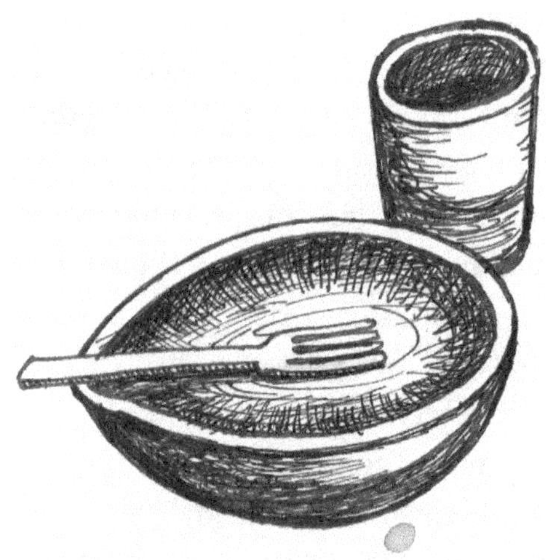

THEASTER GATES'S TABLE: *SOUL FOOD PAVILION*

In 2012 *Soul Food Pavilion* became the vehicle for Theaster Gates to invite folks to the South Side of Chicago to experience the Dorchester Project, which we first encountered in the discussion on place. Gates's orchestration of a Sunday-like dinner, similar to the meal rituals of his upbringing, offers genuine and intimate experiences of home to a wide array of people. Hosted at the Archive House, the events comprised artistic performances, food lessons, and the promise of convivial social exchanges. Moving into a brief description of these items that include the locality, incidentals, rituals, and guests, this chapter proceeds to present an "analysis of intimacy,"[3] a table study that reveals Gates's belief in the material world that mediates the *more* behind feeding people.

Returning to the locality of Dorchester Avenue, guests arrive at the Archive House through a wooden gate made of the same reclaimed lumber that constitutes the house's exterior siding. The entry signals Gates's redemptive habit of upcycling stuff and continues throughout the house. Each rescued fixture stores an origin story, its well-worn attire verifies a history of human contact. For instance, the expanse of plank floorboards attests to many soles traversing its length. The dinks and scrapes of the sentinel shelves divulge their unremitting hold of books and handmade ceramic goods. The main room conveys the clever design of homes featured in *Dwell* magazine, making the space relevant to the aesthete. Concurrent with this minimalist sensibility, constructed furnishings like the built-in benches that double as a makeshift stage communicate a welcoming playfulness produced by frugal ingenuity. The open floor plan plainly states the possibility for revelries, sanctioning human communion. Indeed, the "physical grammar"[4] of Archive House displays a love of place through its eye-catching composition and sensible materiality, which accommodates and expresses hospitality.

Next comes a quick look at *Soul Food Pavilion* incidentals. Tabletop items not only declare Gates's respect and fondness for interesting and beautiful things but also denote his eagerness to share them with others. Stemmed glass goblets promise the tasting of ruby-red wine procured from uncorked bottles. Letterset printed menus on recycled paper are felt announcements that prepare the appetite. Low light and flamed votives evoke a sense of the sacred—setting this meal apart from others. Handmade dinnerware proclaims that each plate, bowl, and cup are just as unique as their beholder. The simplest elements, such as the jute string binding together the eating utensils indicate consideration of the little things. Such visual syntax announces Gates's belief that intentionally selected items help produce tactual experiences that translate as care.

Soul Food Pavilion also offers olfactory pleasures, triggering savory expectations. Guests enjoy a home-cooked meal that consists of catfish, collard greens, and hoecakes. Arranged on specially designed ceramicware made to retain the flavors and forms of soul food, these culinary preparations are meant to recall, commemorate, and redeem historical racial oppressions. A sensible soul food lesson is part of the dinner liturgy that also comprises poetry, dramatic readings, a sermon, and musical performances by Gates's musical ensemble, the Black Monks of Mississippi. Through an atmosphere of amiability, guests are primed to engage in conversations typically avoided at the table, such as God, money, race, power, and politics. Regarding this type of table-talk, it is relevant to consider those seated at Gates's table.

The babble of merged voices that arise from the Archive House declare the relational transactions between Grand Crossing neighbors and Chicago bureaucrats, politicians and social activists, artists and day laborers. Having been seated at Gates's table, art historian Matthew Jesse Jackson confirms the way those on public assistance can be found sharing life stories with uptown millionaires.[5] The allure of locality, food, art, and music contrives proximity meant to convert strangers into friends. By paying careful attention to the aesthetic dimensions of food distribution, Gates applies such graces to support fellowship across social and racial strata. The true beauty of *Soul Food Pavilion* is its ability to level constructed societal divisions. Gates's attentiveness to detail—usually expected by the wealthy—now serves to validate all his guests.

Gates explains the formula that forges such collective cohesion: "When you take the time to make a ritual, then people value the experience. They value the utensils of that experience, and they value the people they meet."[6] By converting dinner into an art medium, place and things collaborate to produce the satisfaction of gathering together. With just this brief assessment of Gates's dinner proceedings, it is possible to detect the multiple feedings at work through *Soul Food Pavilion*.

A TABLE STUDY

Additional analysis of Gates's table manners exposes the capacity of the material to accommodate human interactions, social criticism, and soul work. What is noteworthy about the artist's visceral methodology is its refutation of faith that is interiorized and individualized. It points to the discrepancies between the ideas of Christianity and what is actually practiced. Gates's table preparations enact and substantiate a theology of hospitality that mirrors God's active and visceral hospitality. Thus, Gates's work, and that of artists like him, supplements a type of belief that is overly concerned with dogmatic competence and compliance. It resists a disembodied faith that denigrates the body and blips over its encounters with reality. Instead, faith is nourished through external and cooperative means.

Soul Food Pavilion reveals that constructing a home-like environment roots people to place, houses presence, and spiritually feeds people—some who had yet perceived their hunger. For some, this sounds like church. Indeed, Gates's home-making activities present the ways the sacred can shine through the quotidian. For some Christians, this type of multivalent feeding happens at the Lord's Supper—and it is not accidental.

By reviewing Gates's table from the framework of a theology of hospitality—stewardship, reconciliation, and Spirit revival—the topic eventually turns to the Christian table, mainly but not exclusively the Eucharist, the place-based and spiritual crux of life together. The Christian meal is the subject of the theological portion of the chapter within the construct of ancient Mediterranean banquets. To be sure, both Christ's and Gates's tables exhibit care, connection, and uplifting elements. Both secular and sacred meals also bring to light the way physical things accommodate the intangible need for relationships between God and others.

TABLE STEWARDSHIP

The fact that food is necessary to sustain life makes meal sharing an act of stewardship—caring for others through the distribution of God's provisions. *Soul Food Pavilion's* faithful home-making preparations, its simple, yet hearty, foodstuffs, communicate a number of things: abundance in the ghetto, commentary concerning inaccessibility, and a campaign to conserve a Black American cultural legacy. The dinners exemplify bell hooks's understanding of the Black American need to construct and steward *homeplace*. Through an abundance mentality, homeplace stewardship fights off dehumanizing factors caused by racial injustices.[7]

Gates's South Side of Chicago neighborhood may involve continual experiences of disaffection, but *Soul Food Pavilion* is meant to activate and showcase the wealth within Grand Crossings. Gates contends there is a measure of intentionality concerning economy embedded in Dorchester Avenue hospitality, noting: "I get to ask, along with my neighbors, what does it mean for us to be generous to one another? And what does it mean for us to share the abundance of generosity that we have with other people?" For Gates, making dinner is a big part of collaborative neighborliness.[8] Grounded on the concept of plentitude, the dinners override the privations of the ghetto to feed resilience. Giving away an economic resource like food is a discipline of faith and care that addresses hostilities through acts of hospitality.[9]

Gates's art of neighborliness corresponds to theologian Barbara Holmes's description of a Black American religious life, where the rituals of dinner become the means to sustain persons and invest in joy despite oppressive situations.[10] Remembering her own upbringing amid Gullah families, she recounts that "there was not much money, but there was always a lot of food." Such generosity is defined in terms of a Black contemplative stance, whereby Sunday dinner constitutes a spiritual practice that welcomed guests as family members.[11] Thus the table not only establishes economic sharing but it also negotiates a spiritual act of belonging. Dinner, then, becomes the method to redefine neighbor, friend, or stranger as kin.

The Dorchester Avenue dinners also speak to the flip side of abundance by publicly communicating a Black history of scarcity. The food selection of *Soul Food Pavilion* spells out past injustices that continue into the present. Through his meal-as-art performance, Gates directs guests to the ways the menu items are tokens of subjugation deployed through slave labor and plantation systems. In current times, food disadvantages are exercised through limited distribution of commercial and agricultural goods in poor neighborhoods. Consequently, Gates contends that dinner "actually reveals itself in all these other ways that have nothing to do with eating."[12] By specifically serving and recounting the sources of soul food items and how they were prepared in the fields, Gates dishes out an economy of subsistence to reveal issues of dispossession, systemic racism, and power.

As an art medium, Gates harnesses the corporeal and symbolic realities of dinner. Food is central to the formation of persons. When used as an art form, it brings to light the interplay between persons and their exterior world. Eatables as an art medium depict a "contingency of boundaries" associated with deprivation or accessibility that determines notions of "inside and outside," haves and have nots.[13] As an example, performance theorist Shannon Jackson addresses the antiracist dialogue of artist Pope.L's food performances.[14] His use of processed meal items associated with urban food deserts points to the ins and outs of political, economic, and commercial infrastructures that aggravate health issues in the ghetto. While important, the commentary evoked by Pope.L's smearing of white mayonnaise on his Black body differs vastly from *Soul Food Pavilion*, where Gates's illumination of Black negation brings to light Black American resourcefulness.

Gates moves beyond poverty commentary to further honor the adept stewardship of meager foodstuff by Black Americans. The same belief that resurrects Dorchester Project buildings is now extended to soul vittles through *Soul Food Pavilion*. Gates's guardianship of Black culture now presents collard greens as sacred. He exclaims if, "in five years from now . . . Black people don't make collard greens anymore," then Stony Island Arts Bank will manage "The Center for the Study of Collard Greens."[15] By serving high culinary productions of catfish, hoecakes, and other Southern-enslaved edibles, *Soul Food Pavilion*'s message of economic discrepancies gives way to the distribution and exchange of a cultural legacy.

In addition, Gates's meal art projects open possibilities for various points of human contact. Seeking intercultural correspondence, Gates asks, "If I want to talk about rice a lot, what new friendship might I gain in the cultural sphere?"[16] In this way, rice becomes an emissary that gains traction with other cultures that also eat rice.

An artist's belief in materiality willingly grapples with items' embedded histories, and cultural and symbolic subtilties. For Gates, the life within material substances permits the artist's modest gestures to declare monumental concepts.[17] To this point, the philosopher Gaston Bachelard maintains that artists are phenomenologists who recognize the way items speak. As a consequence of their work, people have better access to the material world.[18] Food, then, as a poetic exchange, challenges others to reevaluate and reinvest in its encumbered social–political realities.

The meals served at *Soul Food Pavilion* events specifically point to slavery and unjust food distribution while simultaneously preserving Black American culinary history. Dinner also provides real sustenance through the miracle of abundance—perhaps akin to the feeding of the five thousand by Jesus. *Soul Food Pavilion*'s stewardship of culture, food, and community also reveals the way Gates's table operates as unifying agent in connection to the reconciliatory stance of a theology of hospitality.

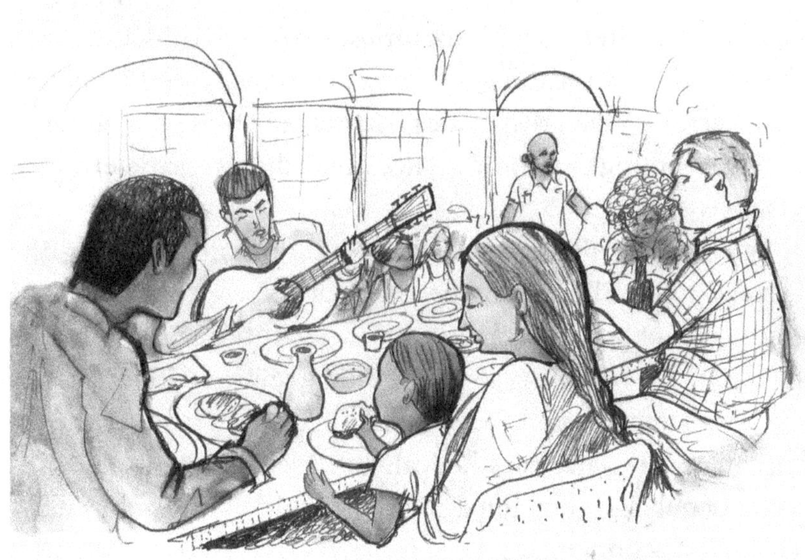

TABLE RECONCILIATION

The universal qualities of the table that corral place, people, and things constitute an apt symbol for the reconciling impetus of a theology of hospitality. Just as it aggregates the beautiful, and the theological, the table also represents the ethical—God's intended justice, where all are invited and seated equi-level. It is an eschatological picture of true homeplace. *Soul Food Pavilion* represents an appealing corporate ceremony where being known and accepted is an important facet of divine reconciliation. Correspondingly, practices of Black American spirituality arise from the pursuit of identity.[19] Black alienation in a white world calls for evocative endeavors grasped through social measures. The alluring intimacy of *Soul Food Pavilion* reflects this impetus to reconcile souls through interpersonal transactions.

Gates maintains that dinner-as-art is a domestically tinged affair "that allows for people to feel safe." He adds that the possibility of closeness gives people "an excuse to become more open, more transparent, more vulnerable." Meal conviviality cements commitments as it celebrates life in spite of indignities. Understanding dinner as a mechanism that merges, Gates directs table discussions involving issues concerning racial disparities. He defends these dialogues as part of dinner, noting that those invited are to discuss predetermined subjects.[20]

Through the difficult mission of equable community building, the Dorchester dinners fill a general need for public/private places where a diverse group of people wrestle with sociopolitical and economic issues. Remarkably, by doing so, they become present to one another. Like the Lord's Supper, *Soul Food Pavilion* becomes a performance of interhuman repair. Gates's aesthetically inclined hospitality expands the format of public discussion directed by ethicists and policy makers. Importing a homeplace logic to such conversations provides a tender approach to hard topics from a nonpropositional stance.

Gates displays that it takes the rituals of the table to inculcate a robust sense of self in the midst of social discomforts, thus enabling reconciling presence.

Playing curator-host, Gates's dinners correspond to Rirtkrit Tiravanija's food performances. Frying up bowls of Pad Thai noodles, Tiravanija relocates cooking and eating to the art space, thereby galvanizing it into a raucous meeting place. As hosts, Gates and Tiravanija enter into the fine art of "invisible social engineering" by constructing social opportunities.[21] This makes people a key ingredient of their art forms. For this reason, critic Miwon Kwon suspiciously construes such hosting as a type of willful socialization. Despite these artists' impetus to democratize, she sees their efforts as deviously authoritarian.[22] In regard to *Soul Food Pavilion*, Kwon's assessment may not be far off. Gates comments that he emulates his mother's dictatorial style of hosting Sunday night dinners. He notes, "Whoever was visiting, if they were a really good singer my ma might say, 'hey, Tawanna, you should get out there and sing a song.'"[23] Gates illuminates that Kwon's critique concerning the tyranny of a host can also be construed as a form of support.

Soul Food Pavilion is grounded on an *oikos* (home) framework that softens authoritarianism through affiliation and affection. Directed by the host, gathered individuals contribute something for the benefit of all. Gates substantiates his own hosting ethos: "Over the years, I've become really sensitive to who's coming to dinner and why they're coming. My hope is that these different folk who meet each other could be friends. And friendship builds a radical encounter. I understood from an early age that dinner could do work besides feeding people."[24] Given Gates's autocrat-host leanings, he admits there is a social agenda behind dinner. He formulates congenial encounters in a society leery of following orders, yet needing safe places to be human, vulnerable, and reliant on the wisdom of others. Gates's meals mediate complex social longings that also address severed race relations. He remarks that his "house is a home, too," adding, "I think that invitation to eat allows for people to cross racial lines and geographic lines that they normally don't cross. And I'm excited about that. There is room and reason to traverse."[25] By way of *Soul Food Pavilion*, healing becomes a *curator*'s purview that pulls together seemingly disparate elements. In Spanish, the word *curar* means to cure.

Soul Food Pavilion embodies what bell hooks terms as "a ritual of belonging,"[26] where eating together fashions an arena for wonderful things to happen. Indeed, Gates reasons that there is a type of beauty that can only be enacted collectively, making *Soul Food Pavilion* "a thing born together."[27] Such collaboration disburses what poet Fred Moten calls "surplus lyricism," explained in relation to jazz improvisation.[28] He categorizes this delivered abundance as *eros*, mutual love that gives birth to *poiema*. Taking this one step toward divine *eros*, the life resulting from rituals of belonging are divine pathways, where "all awakening to love is spiritual awakening."[29] This is because shared effusions of felt love adhere to the standards of "inter-being and interconnectedness."[30] Collaboration necessitates transcendence where the self must reach out and accept another. While themes of love or spirituality are not typically promoted in fine art spaces, Gates, Moten, and hooks defend the way the poetic mediates divinely ordered affection.

THE SPIRIT AND THE TABLE

Spirituality coupled with the notion of *eros* corresponds to the life-giving transactions evident in Gates's work. In preceding chapters, his animating actions were associated with the work of the Spirit, supported by a Black American unified cosmology that permits the quotidian to deliver spiritual truths. A case in point, it has often been expressed that the Spirit that flows through the performing artist also inspires the preacher. "All things draw from the same wellspring of spiritual energy," maintains Holmes.[31] This cohesive spiritual dimension helps explain Gates's monk persona outlined in the last chapter. His hosting habits exhibit the spiritual efficacies of a monk, which honor the mundane and further highlight a ritualistic intelligence.

Gates recognizes that there is a spiritual connection to repetitive measures. As a potter, he terms this pedagogy of the hand as "freaking the pot."[32] Correspondingly, consecutive iterations of making, fixing, cleaning, or cooking promote a pliant body acumen. This type of knowledge is alert, responsive to shifts and changes, creating a channel for the Spirit. Gates's freaking the pot epistemology is also informed by his liturgical experiences as the director of the youth choir at New Cedar Grove Missionary Baptist Church. In this context, souls were informed through fluid improvisations and rhythmic procedures. Hence, *Soul Food Pavilion* depends on the rituals of life, art, faith, and fellowship subsequently displaying the expertise and importance of body receptivity as a conduit for the spiritual.

The altering operations behind such ritualistic gestures, including the Lord's Supper, depend on the polyvalent nature of ritual/aesthetic forms. They function as a learning mechanism by which commitment is roused through a process that stirs conflict, which leads to painful consciousness that further conveys new awareness.[33] Thus, the arts, symbols, rituals, and sacramentality—all these aspects that comprise Gates's meal-sharing events—create tangible experiences that become the location for examination amid defined communal expectations and expressions. Grappling with new information and experiences equips human adaptability. Hence, through rituals, new insights and commitments are garnered.[34] This movement is certainly exemplified in *Soul Food Pavilion*, where Gates as monk releases and extends substances' worth and meaning through the rituals of dinner in order for participants to reevaluate and reinvest in place, people, and material things.

Reading *Soul Food Pavilion* through a Christian lens, dinner's transcendent experiences create a location for divine fellowship as it stewards, reconciles, and revives place, people, and things. This is because whenever persons witness a resounding *yes* to life, such vitality signals that God is present. The impetus to nourish, to heal, to repair is driven by a deep desire for life. The quest is supplied by the hospitable work of the Spirit.[35] Through Christ, the Spirit's presence in the world infuses situations with potentiality, the possibility that new things can occur.[36] This offers a theological explanation for the restorative commitments behind Gates's work,[37] and why he views his endeavors as sacred.

Lastly, as an urban monk, Gates celebrates the divine by helping others enter into the life of material things with its capacity to relate *more*.[38] This ability to illuminate what many fail to see is a movement to resacralize. Gates maintains that "if the material world has the ability to help a person have hope, courage, passion, faith, forgiveness," then the material world is needed to "imagine a more glorious immaterial world." Gates admits that what he seeks "is glory."[39] Christians should likewise practice this type of tangible spiritual labor to spur hope, courage, passion, faith, and forgiveness.

SUMMARY OF *SOUL FOOD PAVILION*

Soul Food Pavilion discloses the material heft and multivalent import of table fellowship. In terms of a theology of hospitality's stance of care and stewardship, Gates's table promotes neighborliness through the application of an abundance theory despite poverty. His dinners also exhibit the effects of food disparities, while simultaneously stewarding the cultural flavors of Black American culinary resourcefulness. In respect to the unifying and reconciling mode of a theology of hospitality, *Soul Food Pavilion* further provides a safe homeplace that affirms Black culture, all the while serving a healthy course of cross-cultural pollination bringing all kinds of people together. Lastly, Gates's table points to the Spirit's renewing work that illuminates the sacred possibilities of place, people, and material things. Gates as monk presents an approach to the divine through a hermeneutic of material reality in order to nourish a secular society starving for meaning and connection. Viewed through the stewarding, reconciling, and vivifying characteristics of a theology of hospitality, Gates's curation of social situations can be understood as a rectifying and connecting mode that wards off multiple levels of isolation as it feeds multiple forms of hunger, for multiple kinds of people.

From the conviviality portrayed in various visual records of *Soul Food Pavilion*, it is easy to apprehend the deep connections being made, the personal stories that are exchanged, and the engaging delivery of historical and present realities of Black American life. The art rouses profound yearnings. In particular, *Soul Food Pavilion* incites a longing for a Christian table that entertains and summons similar ethical meal experiences. Gates's hospitality displays a way for others to likewise arrange delightful homeplaces in order to experience the nurturing, unifying, and vivifying presence of God. Therefore, liturgists, congregational leaders, pastors, Christians, and artists should take note of the way Gates embodies and models hosting habits that ready guests to receive God's unmerited grace. Indeed, if grace is meant to be felt and received, it necessitates real forms, events, and persons.[40] Gates exposes the way spiritual formation necessitates a material world and therefore requires a belief that concrete reality mediates glory.

A THEOLOGY OF HOSPITALITY: JESUS'S TABLE

Describing the *things* that surround Theaster Gates's *Soul Food Pavilion* serves to validate the importance of sensed phenomenon needed for communal, spiritual, and cultural transformation. This is especially necessary to reevaluate Protestant disembodied inclinations that frequently emphasize personal over corporate practices of faith. *Soul Food Pavilion* offers a more holistic and collective approach as it resacralizes place to nourish souls and marshal communal alliances. Moreover, the activity of hosting sets a place for the Holy Spirit to go about its work.[41] Gates's table certainly involves the labor of *feeding* on multiple levels, and so does the Lord's Supper.

Indeed, Gates's meal service cracks open insights into Jesus's own radical hospitality. Jesus inaugurated his own *Soul Food Pavilion*, the distribution of bread and wine to signify his body and blood. The Eucharist—a thanksgiving supper—expresses divine love and commitment as it forms one body from many. Prior to this meal of remembrance, food distribution played a vital role in Jesus's ministry to mediate the kingdom's radical hospitality, entailing diversity and justice.

The aim is to relate the just dimensions between Gates's table and the Lord's Supper. One meal is secular, the other religious. This alone sets the two apart. Indeed, the various theologies and historical legacies that surround the Eucharist and other Christian meals should be enough to discourage any comparison. Nevertheless, the spirituality, cordiality, and ameliorative characteristic of Gates's *Soul Food Pavilion* begs for connection with the Lord's Supper and similar meals. As a visible witness, Dorchester hospitality evokes an enticing eschatological image of the divine banquet depicted by Isaiah where an opulent feast awaits all peoples.

By linking the two tables, the intent is not to minimize the holy elements of the Christian meal. The aim is quite the opposite. As one liturgist puts it, if Christians cannot see the sacred in connection to the ordinary, what does this say about corporate worship and the expectation of God's presence?[42] This chapter explores and promotes a belief in the quotidian, primarily through the material things that surround table fellowship. Exploring Jesus's meals through the lens of *Soul Food Pavilion* gives access to the liminal nature of faith that exists betwixt and between commonplace materiality (place, people, and things) and sacred immateriality (God's gracious commitment to care for, reconcile, and vivify his creation).

THE EUCHARIST AND DIVERSITY

Gates welcomes a wide range of persons as a move to reconcile human divisions. Correspondingly, there is a wide breadth of practices and thought concerning early Christian communal meals, which subsequently advocates for diversity in present acknowledgments concerning the Eucharist—the Christian rite associated with Jesus's final supper with his disciples. Indeed, traditional assumptions that Eucharistic rites originate from a single archetype inculcate universalizing patterns where interpretations or omissions of ancient texts serve to standardize Eucharistic procedures. This occludes, limits, or flattens Christians' responses to grace.

The instructional writings of the *Didache*, the eyewitness accounts of Justin Martyr (Rome, 150) and Ignatius of Antioch (35–108), as well as various meal prayers, show the range and development of Eucharistic meals. The Christian *eucharistia* or blessing (*eulogia*) passages hold similar patterns to Jewish meal prayers (*Birkat ha-mazon, berakah*). Indeed, the word *Eucharist* derives from the very commonplace ritual of giving thanks (*eucharistia*) before a communal meal. Even Jewish liturgical texts and gestures adopted by Christianity were varied. Thus, early Christian meal rituals were, for the most part, pluriform in form and doctrine.[43] The things of the common table bent to the flavors and needs of its practitioners, making table elements geographically and culturally specific. Early Christian meal customs range from ceremonial and symbolic arrangements of the Lord's Supper to more informal *agape* fellowship meals, and sometimes the two are blurred into one. The variety of early Eucharistic forms belie the idea that a single source furnished a unifying influence on later Christian meal rituals.

Another method to resist the traditional assumptions is to analyze texts to extract the power structures behind the *things of* the table in the form of foodstuff. This corresponds to Gates's commentary of dominancy and exclusion expressed through soul food. From baptism meals comprised of milk and honey, to communities that fed on bread and water, to those that excluded wine, or groups that served fruit, cheese, or fish, food signifies its wider social context. There are three identifying impulses behind a community's food choices. Communal meal items were used to (1) declare group distinctiveness, (2) address issues of poverty, or (3) critique sociopolitical power dynamics. Just as the menu of *Soul Food Pavilion* reveals societal inequalities, Christian meal observances express, formulate, and uphold social ideas and structures.[44] Indeed, a table can offer hospitality, but it can equally exclude as it supports governing powers and regulates group distinctions, as seen in the banquet meals depicted in New Testament narratives.

THE BANQUET TABLE

The dining mores of the ancient Mediterranean world reveal the alternative and radical nature of Jesus's table manners. The social dining scenario of the banquet feast, as observed in many New Testament passages, functioned to broker partnerships and advancements that confirmed and retained one's social standing.[45] Within the event, banquet seating further delineated a ranking system. For instance, those found luxuriously reclining signaled their status as free male citizens. If social meals are to be understood as manifestations of societal hierarchies that further perpetuate a culture's worldview, then the exclusion of women, slaves, foreigners, and children from meal events reveals their impotency in the game of alliance keeping.[46] Such exclusions and class stratifications differed from Christianity's radical hospitality where Greek and Jew, free and slave, men and women dined together.

Despite the banquet's delineated social aims, it models the way *the things* of the table prove to be valuable incidentals toward achieving group consensus. Similar to *Soul Food Pavilion*, the ancient Mediterranean banquet consisted of an eating portion, followed by a symposium. The latter provided an exchange of cultural goods (art, music, dance, and poetry) and ideas in the form of philosophical discussions that further cemented group identity and ethos.[47] The banquet also held a religious dimension. Throughout the evening, wine libations were offered to the gods as participants imagined themselves seated at a heavenly table.

This differs from the Lord's Supper, which subverts the banquet cosmology. At the earthbound Christian table, participants find themselves in communion with God and each other by way of Jesus's body.[48] Through the Spirit, all have access to food and fellowship. Such radical inclusion exudes a quality that Gates rightly defines as sacred. *Soul Food Pavilion* certainly displays the way this combination of goods holds potential toward commitment building that further signals the moral significance of hosting.[49]

TABLE DIVISIONS

The physicality of shared meal rituals sustains the fabric of society. Just as the banquet meals communicate status and thus reveal who is welcomed at the table, Christian meal gatherings convey differing notions of worthiness. Throughout church history, distributional patterns of Eucharistic meals have spiritually fed people while also establishing ecclesial hierarchies. Depending on a church's sacramental view determines who dispenses the meal and who partakes. Accordingly, the Eucharist may physically represent Christ's body or operate as a symbolic act of remembrance—with a spectrum of convictions in between. Allocation of bread and wine may dispense divine forgiveness, while grape juice and crackers simply point to Christ's sacrificial love. A fence that limits participation may guard the sanctity of elements or keep it within the family, while an open table becomes an opportunity to feed all who are hungry and thirsty. These polemics of belief reveal the way Christ's table has become for some a place of division, discord, and injustice.

The ability to control Eucharistic fare, whether through banning, distribution, or moderation, represents the governance of other aspects of life as well.[50] Such management shapes and visibly projects ecclesial structures and ordinances communicating to certain members and visitors whether they belong or are held suspect. In turn, the blessed continue to receive hospitality, while the rejected must seek it elsewhere.

The things surrounding a meal will manifest the attitudes of its servers—their brokenness and glory. Indeed, the diverse and divergent practices and interpretations of fellowship meals, accrued throughout history, reveal the elasticity, depth of meaning, and grace of the Christian table. Whether it is the Eucharist, an *agape* meal, or fellowship banquet, it is important for Christians to realize the ways physical things like locality, food stuff, seating arrangements, utensils, and dinner attendants can support homeplace or deny it. Religious communities should consider their food practices and surrounding texts and gestures, noting what they communicate to participants, guests, and neighbors. With humility, all Christians should be mindful of their own dinner preparations, remembering the agency a meal offers.

JESUS'S TABLE

It takes the hospitable, convivial activities of Theaster Gates's table to expose the reconciliatory aspect of *koinōnia* (fellowship or participation) belonging to Jesus's ethical table. The image of the poor and rich dining together portrayed in *Soul Food Pavilion* corresponds to Jesus's alternative hospitality within the closed social systems of both the ancient Mediterranean world and current Eucharistic customs. Luke 14 establishes Jesus's inclusive strategies embedded in the stories shared at a Pharisee's table, and the apostle Paul's well-known admonishment displays the exclusionary acts of rich Christians seated at the Corinthian table. Both passages reveal a theology of hospitality's nurturing quality that crosses into the reconciliatory mode to establish a just and united table that accommodates many.

As a religious rite, the Eucharist can point to the spiritual benefits of general meal sharing. This expands ideas of eating as a spiritual discipline beyond following dietary laws. The biblical narratives involving distribution or reception of food can be symbolic of grace, God's care for creation.[51] Indeed, both Luke and Acts shift the topic of eating from religious prohibition to kingdom provision. Whether it is Jesus's disciples picking heads of grain on the Sabbath, the post-resurrection revelatory meal at Emmaus (outside of the temple city), or Peter's vision of new food allowances, the triune God looks to physically, socially, and spiritually nourish all types of people. Such maintenance exposes the reconciliatory nature of Jesus's ministry that utilizes food as a means to negotiate God's forgiveness. Consequently, Luke's table tales point to ultimate reconciliation imaged as the eschatological Messianic table where all nations, languages, and tribes dine together.[52] Gates's lively and equitable approach established in *Soul Food Pavilion* offers a foretaste of such a feast.

Such impartial favor is not the case at the Pharisee's table in Luke 14. Here, the gospel writer depicts a meal where Jesus communicates a cluster of table stories ending with the feast that welcomes the prodigal son in Luke 15. All are meant to paint a portrait of Jesus's radical hospitality that simultaneously comments on the reciprocal benefit paradigm of the banquet meal, which is now embedded into the Sabbath celebration of the Pharisee. Jesus's first gesture is inspired by a guest suffering from water retention. Despite religious regulations against work, the man with dropsy is healed at the Sabbath table, pointing to the transformational possibilities of hosting. Following this lesson, in which physical parchedness signals its spiritual equivalent, Jesus responds to the competitive dash between guests seeking to grab the most prestigious seating options—a physical detail that specifically portrays the situation's social hierarchies. With sage-like authority, Jesus teaches that kingdom honor is not apprehended through expectant social exchanges but is obtained through grace—regardless of where one sits. He continues to sketch out the table ethos of the new age with the parable of a wealthy host.

His lesson depicts a rich man who sends dinner invitations to his peers. Citing their busyness with new capital ventures, the group of urban elites decline the offer. Apparently, their recent acquisitions of land, cattle, and marriage dowry present a more compelling economic advantage than the networking benefits of the proposed banquet party. To guarantee attendees, the host sends out a second set of invitations to the lame and sick. This group holds little leveraging power as they are mainly unemployed, and thus able to attend the festivities. Having more room for guests, the host distributes a third round of requests to those outside the city. This group represents the rural poor, or outsiders in general.[53] Consequently, Jesus's parable advocates a table that seats the sick, the poor, and the alien. Like Gates, Luke is concerned with who gets to sit at the table and depicts the way Jesus strays from mono-social strategies evidenced by Greco-Roman social practices.

Through the parable, Jesus offers an alternative set of qualifications for kingdom-building fellowship—the rich can invite and mingle with those unable to transfer any social or material advantages. Indeed, like the healing of the man with dropsy at the top of the narrative, Luke illustrates the way Jesus's table is transformational as the rich man also undergoes conversion. The host could have easily turned the banquet into a charity soup kitchen. Instead, by choosing the role of convivial host, the rich man initiates kingdom *koinōnia* by setting a table that is inclusive, honors the marginalized, and challenges the social games of the upwardly mobile.[54] By way of this story, Jesus illuminates the way a table can operate as a level playing field that visually displays God's hospitality. Here, joy, beauty, care, and camaraderie are extended to all people, regardless of society's ideas of fame, shame, patronage, or honor.[55] As portrayed in the New Testament, Jesus eats with all kinds of people—rich, religious, outcasts, and sinners. Within the auspices of a theology of hospitality, his table manners enable many to experience God's love. This makes the table the site of reconciliation, as suggested by the story of the prodigal son. The father opens his arms to receive his wayward son(s), thus ending the Lucan pericope about meals. From the Pharisee's house to the father's plea, Luke poses an invitation for all, asking, Will you sit and celebrate at the new kingdom table?[56]

THE RECONCILIATION OF THE CORINTHIAN TABLE

Paul's letter to the church at Corinth is also concerned with the way the Christian table displays kingdom values. As Luke's witness portrays, the table is the site for social leveling. Yet at Corinth, Paul observes the way the rich perpetuate social disparities through their unchecked table manners. They joyously fill themselves with food, while others remain hungry (1 Corinthians 11:20–21). If, according to Paul, sharing bread and cup is meant to portray Christian *koinōnia* (literally "joint sharing"),[57] then unequal food distribution signals a regress to the social strategies of pagan banquet rites. This divide falsifies the unifying principle of the Lord's Supper, and thus weakens its observable *kerygmatic* character.

Unlike the Greco-Roman banquet event that conferred and confirmed a place in the prevailing social stratum, Christians were to enact and visibly portray the eschatological significance of unity through diversity at Christ's table. Here, space is reserved for gentiles, women, slaves, strangers, and also for the broken and the sinner.[58] Within God's new order, old social distinctions are jumbled. Just as Gates's neighbors serve modest cuisine to the elite, and the host in the Lucan parable dines with outsiders, Paul invites Corinth's privileged Christians to hold back and set a just table. The substantiality of a meal also combats Gnostic attitudes concerning the spiritual gifts of the new age (for both the Corinthians and present-day Christians).

Thanks to Theaster Gates, there is an existing model that amplifies Jesus's radical hospitality. Inculcated through the *koinōnia* of Gates's family's table and arguably the Christian table, Gates's *Soul Food Pavilion* is an efficacious witness, a way to reevaluate and honor impoverished lives.[59] By setting a table as an art piece, Gates creates a just system for all to receive God's nourishment. Whether Gates's or Jesus's table, the Spirit enables true connection.

SPIRIT AND TRANSCENDENCE

It is the work of the Spirit that primes people to encounter *more*. Such openness enables human transcendence—advancing beyond the self to accept what is other. Human transcendence is grounded in God's hospitality, the divine movement to embrace place, people, and things. There is a strain of Christian thought that has emphasized God's otherness—godly transcendence from the world. Yet, the value of communicating divine alterity has garnered a disaffected view of creation and its materiality. If Jesus is always a host, even when a guest at the table, then the theological idea of God's transcendence is not a move away from corporeality but one that favors intimacy with the things of this world.

Divine transcendence is directed toward creation. In light of *imago Dei* to *missio Dei* performances explored in the last chapter, the triune God's economic transactions inform the way humanity is to reach beyond the self to choose love. Indeed, God reverences Godself by honoring what has been created. In other words, God's perfect triune union need not care, reconcile, or enliven creation.[60] But these undertakings do comprise the way God honors the Godself through a surplus flow of love that pours divine presence into the world by way of the Spirit. This spiritual transaction reaches its apogee at the site of the trinitarian table.[61] The Lord's Supper signals the way Jesus honors God with his physical body. Here, Christ's sacrifice allows those who are not God to commune with the divine.

By way of the Spirit, the Lord's Table is where God's love becomes accessible and tangible through multiple significations of Christ's body. God's radical self-giving offers the spiritual means for humans to likewise be for the other, to be just, and love all bodies. It is at Eucharistic tables that Christians remember and practice that they are restored to God for the benefit of one another.[62]

This makes the Lord's Supper the place to rehearse human transcendence—to move from alienation into community. *Koinōnia* is embodied love, displayed at an actual table, consequently making Christ immanent by the Spirit.[63] As Theaster Gates's *Soul Food Pavilion* demonstrates, meal sharing is one way to perform a kinship ethos that also impels a commitment to care for, reconcile, and vivify creation. Sensible table hospitality is a future-oriented operation, a practice run for the great feast to come.[64] As table hosts, believers serve a meal informed by Christ's sacrificial *kenosis*, the pouring out of self. For this reason, the wine served at the Lord's Supper differs from the drink libations of the Greco-Roman banquet table. Banquet wine aimed to seat participants with the gods. The implication here is that they were to be honored like the gods. However, the Lord's Table signals the way Christ empties himself of his divine rights to enter into the travails and joys of being human. God honors Godself by liberating humanity from having to play God, yet they can now partake of divine communion as God's guests.

CONCLUSION

At Gates's table, spirituality is supplied through food service to portray the physical properties of faith. This enlarges a materialist view by crediting the *more* to *things*. Yet Gates's glorification of objects also pokes at a gnostic spirituality that turns its back on material culture. In a similar turn, Paul refutes the Gnosticism of the Corinthian table. By utilizing the image of the human body, Paul substantiates Spirit work, highlighting its concrete manifestations, the exercise of individuals' gifts for community building. We see this at Gates's table when those seated are invited to share a little bit about themselves, thus enacting human transcendence.

The solidity of Gates's *Soul Food Pavilion* reveals a wealth of meaning and experiences distributed through the rituals of setting a beautiful table. Dinner-as-art embodies and represents a way to steward an abundance economy dependent on neighborliness. It addresses power and racial disparities, and redeems cultural food fare. Through the Black sacred cosmos of Black American spirituality, Gates models a holistic approach to faithful hosting where a liturgy of preparing, serving, and eating food binds together a group of diverse people.[65] Such labors make dinner a spiritual affair that deepens the worth of place, people, and material things.

Soul Food Pavilion also reminds believers of the core values connected to the Lord's Supper. With his body, Jesus realizes an eschatological feast where all nations are represented. What is more, *Soul Food Pavilion* points to the way Christ's Spirit empowers all Christians to set a just table that further resists all types and degrees of alienation. Home making through the delectable qualities of meal fellowship demonstrates a generous hospitality where dinner "actually reveals itself in all these other ways that have nothing to do with eating."[66]

4

Home Making

> "The earth is the LORD's, and all that is in it, the world, and those who live in it."
>
> —Psalm 24:1 (NRSV)

> "We do this because it's the closest we can get to God . . . Since we don't go to church anymore, we don't experience the holy ghost, we don't eat together on Fridays. . . . All of the things that have been the conventions of a collective emotion, we don't have them anymore. All we have is brunch . . . in the absence of the temple, art is all we got."
>
> —Theaster Gates[1]

The triune God fashions a cosmos tinged with welcoming domesticity, arranging heaven and earth as home. Creation, then, bears the marks of divine hospitality. Genesis testifies to creation's rhythmic ordering, inaugurating a biblical theology of hospitality, in which God's homemaking and keeping declare a divine ethos of welcome and embrace. From the first garden to the final temple, God desires to make a home for us and with us. Throughout these pages, hospitality has been explored through a framework of three divine qualities: covenantal stewardship, just coherence that spawns interconnectivity throughout the diverse spectrum of God's creation, and the animating function of hospitality that restores place, people, and material things.[2] In an artful manner, Gates conveys aspects of God's inviting character through correlating acts of care, reconciliation, and revival.

In Greater Grand Crossings, where the Dorchester Project is situated, the artist's home-making methodology brings about sociospatial possibilities, which further relate his place-based commitments articulated as belief. Such neighborhood preservation tactics communicate abundance in the ghetto, soul transformations through the poetic, and the redemption of "lesser value things" as they are relocated to "a space of absolute value."[3] With inflections of the local, the artist's activities on the South Side of Chicago establish sacred places where God's hospitality is extended.[4]

Yet the Dorchester Project is also a critical response to an instrumentalist and capitalist view of land management that excludes, exploits, and establishes inequities. As a counter movement, Gates takes a civic-minded approach to property ownership. His redevelopment strategies consider the social and cultural dimensions needed to support community, which shifts an undistinguished resident into a neighbor. Because Gates's real-estate tactics complement the community development energies of Black American religious groups, they provide a window to view a model of faith and work integration. Responding to the debilitating effects of racial injustices, many Black churches rejected private–public differentiation to implement social countermeasures such as job training, housing, financial assistance, loan programs, educational opportunities, and more. Biblically, these home-making deeds correspond to Israel's stewardship of place. Offerings from the land were to be gathered and redistributed by Israel as a conduit of God's grace to neighboring nations.

In the guise of a monk, Gates reinvigorates this biblical view of home making as a spiritual act. His belief in place is continuous to his belief in people. Through the 2010 exhibition *To Speculate Darkly*, Gates's artistic performances advance a type of hospitality that cares for, reconciles, and revives souls. Throughout the Milwaukee Art Museum's exhibition, Gates honors the resilience and beauty of Black labor by highlighting the creative work of antebellum enslaved potter Dave Drake. This poet-potter stands as a universal icon for all marginalized persons. Subsequently, both Gates's and Drake's labors represent the ways artistic production becomes a pathway to resist dehumanizing forces for all people. Through the exhibition's creative collaborations, Gates exposes the ways art mediates possession of the self, affirms an epistemology of making, and constructs a monumental place whereby the poetic provides a tangible presence others must negotiate. Fueled by a belief that all people matter, *To Speculate Darkly* depicts bodies in motion as a method to navigate debilitating grievances. The result is poetic progress that symbolizes the achievable.

The operations that comprise *To Speculate Darkly* correspond to the theological movement of *imago Dei* to *missio Dei*. Mission of God activities challenge the hostilities that tarnish the image of God status of all humans. Art production is one such maneuver. For this reason, theologian Willie Jennings encourages churches to invest in the *imago Dei* creativity of its members. Adopting this iconic logic supplies transformative experiences that bind people together, mediate communion with God, and subvert a dominating white aesthetic by tendering new images of faith.[5] Such an artistic ecclesial program would broaden, display, celebrate, and mirror the multiple and varied expressions of God's creativity expressed throughout creation and culture.

In turn, an iconic logic critiques and corrects a Western Christianity depicted and disseminated globally through visions of the good life presented by white bodies. Jennings's prescription, and Gates's manifested belief, release many from measuring themselves to a white aesthetic. Such strategies exemplify tenets of liberation theology, which promote, gather, and investigate images, stories, cultural objects, and gestures of the marginalized to decolonize persons and communities, really everyone, from the dictums of white supremacy.[6] These emancipatory methods are grounded in God's hospitality, which fashions earth-as-home and populates it with nations, tribes, peoples, and languages.

The prophet Isaiah depicts this diverse multitude sitting at a table where a feast of fine foods and aged wine is served to all peoples, making dinner the apparatus to deliver divine grace (Isaiah 25:6–7). The prophet's vision is manifested in *Soul Food Pavilion*, a series of meal performances that represent the importance of material reality to convey radical hospitality. Fed by the rituals of family and church, Gates's home-making efforts express the postures of love and hope so needed today. To be sure, *Soul Food Pavilion* delineates the way art, food, and conversation arbitrate interpersonal transcendence made possible by fashioning safe environs. Consequently, this chapter extols a belief in the material world needed to access the immaterial.

Gates's convivial and just hosting habits reveal the heart of God's hospitality, where place, people, and material culture convene and are relished. Yet, *Soul Food Pavilion*, like the meal narratives in Luke, also brings to light the power dynamics behind food distribution. Analysis of Gates's table provides entry into Jesus's radical hospitality that counters Greco-Roman dining conventions. At Gates's and Jesus's table, the tangibility of food stuff provides a vehicle for all kinds of people to experience God's beauty, provision, and justice. Meal fellowship is a receptacle that welcomes the corporeality of God's creation as a conduit of divine revelation.[7] Whether a table is set as an art form, religious ritual, or at home, its materiality permits communion with God, earth's bounty, and others to refresh souls.

Surveying Gates's substantial expressions of belief expands the subject matter for Christians to engage a cultural hermeneutic. The analysis authorizes the theological import of art, as well as discounted theological perspectives needed to reanimate segments of fossilized Christianity. Advocating hospitality as a theological prospect is necessary to shift belief beyond Protestantism's interiorization and lessen an Enlightenment preoccupation of conforming the will. To mainly rely on an inward reception of faith and distrust corporeality only serves to disconnect from God's world, which subsequently generates hostilities toward certain places, people, and material realities. Gates, on the other hand, teaches that place making, performing, and food preparation *embody* a theology of hospitality.

REVISITING PLACE, PEOPLE, AND MATERIAL THINGS

The Dorchester Project, *To Speculate Darkly*, and *Soul Food Pavilion* reveal Gates's monastic labors that permit critical reflection, community, and social transformations. Gates's poetic activities hold sacred dimensions as they engender obligations, bring about cohesion, and look to restore what matters to God. In a society marked by indifference, divisions, and hostilities, the porous and fluid nature of spirituality and the poetic are essential to interrelations.

An example of Gates's place-based interventions comprised of sacred elements is the 2015 installation *Sanctum*. Inside the bombed-out ruins of Temple Church in Bristol, England, Theaster Gates constructed a chapel-like structure and activated the space with 522 hours of nonstop sound performances featuring area musicians and performers. The artist explains that *Sanctum* was meant to be "a platform on which the people of Bristol have an opportunity to hear each other."[8] Similar to the home-making methods that restored and converted the abandoned properties of the Dorchester Project, *Sanctum* salvaged building components from former Bristol factories and churches—the places where folks gathered to work and pray—to represent the way neighborliness weaves the ecologies of locality to leverage sociability.

Gates shows how sacred spaces are needed to sustain his belief in people. In the case of the 2018 exhibition *Black Madonna* at Kunstmuseum Basel, Gates specifically validates and memorializes Black femininity. Through careful curation, a visual conversation commenced between the museum's holdings, the religious cult of the Black Madonna, and glossy photo images of beautiful Black women pulled from the magazine archives of *Ebony* and *Jet*. *Black Madonna* is the means for Gates to elevate the prominence of women in religious history,[9] recognize the connections between Black spiritual and political power, and indicate his own personal context of growing up the youngest and only male out of nine children. Gates recounts, "I was super-interested in how powerful women in and around my life seem to be a solution that the world is never looking for."[10] In many ways, *Black Madonna* broadens concepts from *To Speculate Darkly* by providing a feminine counterpart to Dave Drake. The fashion photographs speak to the power of aesthetics in the popular sphere, enabling all women to imagine their iconic worth. A Womanist theological analysis of various Black Madonna religious icons found throughout Europe would give voice to the struggles, judiciousness, strengths, and faith of Black women as they care for those they love.[11] Both exhibitions portray figures that have been disinherited from *imago Dei* status.

Helping others to find their poetic potential is one way Gates expresses his belief in people. Giving folks in poor neighborhoods access to cultural experiences is the reason why he developed the Arts Bank in Grand Crossings, which became a laboratory for the Arts + Public Life space developed through his director role with the University of Chicago. He asks, "How do you create bigger platforms that don't just benefit one person, they start to benefit a whole bunch of people?"[12] Another of his immediate solutions is his yearly retreat for Black artists. Establishing the program provides encouragement, networking, aesthetic explorations, and enrichment for Black artists to thrive.

In the category of Gates's belief in material things, *Soul Food Pavilion* displayed the poetic use of material objects to plunge viewers into historical, cultural, and religious matters. The same is true of his adoption of a gazebo associated with Tamir Rice. Amid the Black Lives Matter movement, after organizations in Cleveland declined to care for the gazebo, Tamir's mother, Samaria Rice, contacted Gates. Gates took on a liturgical approach when he accepted custody of the garden structure connected to the shooting of the twelve-year-old child by police officers. Just as the *things* that surround meal fellowship negotiate justice and love, Gates's preservation of the gazebo and its collected mementos provides a means to examine the crisis of a country in the midst of racial, political, and economic despair. As a shrine, the material presence of the memorial mediates fear, grief, and anger inflamed by unnecessary police force upon Black lives. Gates relates that the gazebo provides a concrete location that offers people "a chance to mourn."[13] The Rice gazebo shelters collective emotions and perhaps functions as a canopy that stretches over acts of forgiveness and justice.

ART AND THEOLOGY *EN CONJUNTO*

Sanctum, Black Madonna, and the Tamir Rice gazebo represent imaginative reconfigurations of neighborliness harmonious with the triune God's performance of care, reconciliation, and revival. Poet Aja Monet decrees, "hospitality defies sin."[14] The procedure of exploring art and theology from the margins certainly aims to defy sins that exclude. Alongside the authority of an artist that imparts Black home-making experiences, Hispanic/Latinx liberation theology's *en conjunto,* or conjoining method, also supports the anthropological approach of offering lived occurrences to deepen abstract theological assessments.[15] *En conjunto* presents an integrative and practical theology that revives people, cultural expressions, and elements of God's creation as a source for shaping new identities and communities. *En conjunto,* theology done in/for community, enables a poetic theology that heeds human yearnings for home and belonging.

As a theological mode concerned with Christian practices, *en conjunto* is an anthropological method that steers Christian attention to seemingly secular and prosaic affairs. Divine hospitality is always at work, whether Christians are paying attention or not. Therefore, God cannot be sectioned off into certain corners of life.[16] *Teologia en conjunto* takes into account the mutual relationship between secular and sacred to address the human condition and make sense of various experiences of the good. This brings to mind the way Gates portrays the monk archetype explicit in *Black Monastic* performances (chapter 2) as he provides alternatives to race/class-restricted living by way of spirited cultural production.[17] A renewed discipleship model emerges by unpacking Gates's performances in light of God's unfolding purposes for the world.

A theology of hospitality follows God's home-making rhythms throughout creation and culture as a viable source for faith, practice, and theological reflection. Through Christ's Spirit, human home-making responds to, participates in, and echoes the renewing force of divine housekeeping.

Gates provides safe places to express human foibles and needs. He understands that repair is possible by acknowledging wrongdoing. As a student of religion, and as a former worship director, Gates observes the mechanisms of religious rituals that mediate human drama. He employs them in the public square, identifying that, for many, church is not their reality. He explains, "We do this because it's the closest we can get to God. . . . Since we don't go to church anymore, we don't experience the holy ghost, we don't eat together on Fridays. . . . All of the things that have been the conventions of a collective emotion, we don't have them anymore. All we have is brunch . . . in the absence of the temple, art is all we got."[18] Certainly, transformation occurs in church pews, but also in the row seating of cinemas, theaters, and concert halls.[19] The spiritual framework of awakening, purgation, illumination, and union is activated in museums and galleries. This secular sacredness does not signal the end of Christendom but its restoration. Artists like Gates can stimulate the Christian imagination to forge new paths to faith, and incite reexamination of traditional forms of communal practices to extend Christ's radical hospitality.

LIMITATIONS OF ART AND THEOLOGY CONJUNCTION

While promoting the program of comingling art and theology as a means of exposing God's involvement with creation, there are limitations involved with such proceedings. On the art side, viewing art pieces through a theological lens imposes certain notions never intended by the artist. To specifically conjoin Gates's endeavors with a theology of hospitality holds the danger of limiting its capacity to orient participants to important and valid social, political, and economic agendas circumscribed by the artist. The art for art's sake axiom is a firmly held conviction that defends a work's autonomy against instrumentality. This is exactly why, in light of postmodernity's preoccupation with power and domination, suspicion arises concerning coercive aims in connection with religion and art. Still at play is the important avant-garde agenda that art's aim is to interrupt or shift viewer's perceptual assumptions to incite contemplation of human affairs. For this reason, traditional art philosophies reject the ameliorative dimensions of some social practice art projects because the aesthetic-beneficial dimension is seen as a form of instrumentation that can undercut the critical nature of contemporary art.

Gates has something to say about these strictures. First, within his holistic framework, art can disrupt *and* provide remedy. For this reason, Gates does not self-designate as a social practice artist, mainly because he feels that the "s" of social practice art is too little. "What if the 's' got bigger?" he asks. "Could the artist consider herself inside a bigger problem?" On the matter of cojoining the analysis of other discourses to his work, Gates contends that "we are sometimes too one-to-one: art history-to-artist." He advocates an art criticism that broadens its purview to take into account the "religious scholar" or "a housewife, or a roofer, or a fireman" as the means to comprehend and appreciate the work, while also providing a different "way of entering."[20] Indeed, the communicative and performative properties of social practice art incite a process of responsive exchanges.[21] This offers some room for theological participation concerning socially engaged art forms like the ones presented by Theaster Gates.

Despite obtaining the artist's permission to approach his work from a theological position, the discourse of theology holds its own prescribed approaches. There is a good amount of literature that engages art simply as a means to illustrate theological concepts. Still, other approaches engage art in a comparative or dialogical manner whereby the poetic is placed next to theology to allow for a conversation that would influence both spheres yet never interpolate.[22] While boundaries are evident and necessary, this type of bifurcation tends to mask interrelationships. It further denies notions of contact, permeability, and communion between art, faith, and real-life circumstances.

Another anxiety pertinent to exploring art forms as *loci theologici* concerns certain Protestant theological positions that question divine revelation through the created and cultivated world, while a critique of liberation theology mistrusts reflection from anthropological perspectives and its ever-shifting situations. Theological exploration concerning secular art forms must also contend with conflicting language and aims that include ambiguous notions of the sublime.

While art may not exercise salvific power, or pass any purity tests, it does participate in bringing about transformation. Theologically, this elicits a series of questions on the nature of transcendence. If abiding moments that arise out of art-aesthetic experiences are not linked to the God of the Bible, do they hold any worth toward Christian formation or deserve theological attention? If Gates's practice alludes to a vague or general sense of the divine, does this disqualify it from operating as an avenue to comprehend the particulars of the Judeo-Christian faith? What is more, many are uncomfortable with contemporary art's open-ended and obscure manner. It is certainly disconcerting for those who approach the poetic in terms of the propositional looking for hard data.

HOSPITALITY FROM THE MARGINS

While some of the objections belonging to both discourses are valid, a theology of hospitality—remembering God as ultimate host of creation—supports the integrative aspect of theology and art from the margins. Everything belongs to God. Consequently, this study summons the work of artists, liberation theologians, and other scholars concerned with issues of race and displacement to talk about divine hospitality, with the hope of fostering Christian hospitality. Philosopher Emmanuel Levinas communicates hospitality/hostility in terms of *beingness* wrapped in the modern era's fears of usurpation, which emerged from Europe's crisis concerning the historical fall of long-held empires and subsequent drawing up of national lines that heightened issues of ethnicity. The succeeding world wars further engineered modes of isolation to display the way *beingness* engendered "acts of repulsing, exiling, stripping, killing." The ethical response is to consider the face of the *Other* as a way to prompt accountability concerning ethnic, racial, and national identities.[23] While Levinas seeks the face, the philosopher Jacques Derrida singles out the voice of the stranger. "The one who, putting the first question, puts me in question," he declares, seeing the critical role of the foreigner as that of an embodied question mark.[24] The stranger's unfamiliarity with locality calls into question customs, and in doing so shakes assumptions, disrupting the way things are normally done. The stranger, then, provokes crisis, yet can also open new horizons.[25] This conversation offers insight to Gates's hospitality: like a stranger, his art interrogates as a way to advance hospitality, also revealing the complexities of hospitality as it carries the twin possibilities of human vulnerability and violence. Hosts and guests can interchangeably behave as foe. The host can restrict, and the alien is capable of displacing the host.[26]

The Latin root word of hospitality is *hospes,* which signifies host or guest. In the Gospel narratives, Jesus simultaneously incarnates both roles. Thereby, his followers must also rely on *and* practice Christ's hospitality.[27] The cruciform life is one of exposure and openness. It is an anthropological project of hospitality, divinely hosted.

If given a voice at the table, those from diasporic, immigrant, and mestizo communities offer perceptions that question the superiority of the West. Having to navigate multiple cultural realities, outsiders challenge ideas of self-reliance, detachment, and dualisms. Treated as perpetual guests, and disqualified by terms like illegal, illogical, and inferior, the hospitality received from those alienated serves to feed an anemic Western *beingness.* Theology and aesthetics from the margins resist modernity's biases, its splintering of societal and vocational spheres, ethnic and racial divisions, and epistemic hierarchies. In addition, relying on "worldly theologies" assists in apprehending the holistic operations of people of color concerning spiritual and religious life.[28]

Indeed, studying Gates's work provides the ability to survey segments of Black American church practices. What is glimpsed is a comprehensive way of life where belief is publicly displayed through social, aesthetic, political, proprietor, economic, and religious means. "To be re-created by God in and through the life of the church involves all of who we are," exclaims theologian Elizabeth Newman. Liturgical operations release participants to be "transformed" into "vehicles for God."[29] Thus the body operates as a hinge that connects various aspects of life to affect the home (*oikos*), ethics (*ethos*), and community (*polis*).[30]

For Gates in particular, the conjoined power of art and spirituality assists in countering a disposition that bifurcates spirit and materiality, and shuns public displays of emotion. The artist's strategies exert migration patterns that readily unify Western binaries that split public/private, secular/sacred, profit/nonprofit, art/life, and art/theology. Gates's alternative is to weave these items together to determine himself as "a full-time artist, a full-time urban planner, and a full-time preacher with an aspiration of no longer needing any of those titles."[31] His work offers a way to acknowledge the points of contact between faith and art experiences grounded by God's unifying shalom as housekeeper. Gates's art, and that of other social practice artists, opens a place within liberation theology where Christian artists can explore, employ, and embody critique, while simultaneously caring for many. This type of theo-poetic practice points to the unifying principle of a theology of hospitality that indicates the interconnectedness of God's earth, its inhabitants, and everything in it. Here, the Spirit permits differentiation (as the ordering in Genesis 1 represents) and enables permeability that allows for associations in the manner of Christ's human-divine concurrence.

SPIRIT LIFE: *ORTHOPATHOS*

The conjoined life of Christ expresses the potency of the Spirit that supports interrelations. That which is Spirit *and* Divine Other takes on flesh and enters a family, a tribe, a nation. Theology from the margins expressed through a Black sacred cosmos, or *en conjunto* method, *mujerista*, or *mestizo* mode presents religious orientations that interact with persons from a kin approach. Theologian Samuel Solivan terms this kind of engagement as *orthopathos* as it denotes an inclination toward neighbor that compels responsibility.[32] Indeed, the Spirit finds a receptacle in social interactions. Such abiding occasions are operational in Black church sanctuaries, as well as embodied as a "spiritual idea" shaped by the Scriptures, history, stories, and the myths of subjugated people.[33] For this reason, the term *spiritual* moves beyond church structures to comprise a sacred mode where, in the quest to defy alienation, abiding moments are constantly pursued in *all* parts of shared life: church, family gatherings, work, and artistic gestures like dance, song, and stories.[34]

Gates speaks of this type of religious orientation according to his parents' belief. Unlike traditional Christian theology, which is used as a tool to dominate and enslave, Gates found that liberation theology helped to reevaluate Jesus according to the perceivable faith practices of those around him. "What I knew was that God was a God of hope, love, and compassion. The God of my mother and father was different from the God of the Spaniards," remarks Gates of his family's observable faith.[35]

The cherishing, *abiding* approach conveyed through Gates's art models the way hosting can be the domain of the Spirit. This corresponds to a theological approach that views the Spirit as person. When the Spirit's subjectivity is acknowledged, it further permits human worth and agency, especially for those who are frequently treated as nonpersons.[36]

Empowerment is another way to understand the Spirit's activity correlative to the arts. Gates explains the interrelationship by commenting that he is "a believer in transformative acts." Not just turning clay into a vessel but also "the kind of Holy Ghost transformations" that commence "when we start singing a song and we keep singing that song, and then we all find ourselves transforming the space around us because the music is doing the thing both internally and externally."[37] Correspondingly, there exists an "abiding connection" between artistic communication and God's move toward us through material means by way of the Holy Spirit.[38] This is why Jennings's iconic logic (chapter 2) advocates a church's investment in its artistic potentialities as a way to navigate empathy and emotions, which further fosters commitment to one another.

Orthopathos

Solivan's term *orthopathos*—the holy arena of emotions and empathy—is relevant to a home-making theology. Besides holding a theological traditional framework of orthodoxy (right belief) and orthopraxis (right practice) to establish right relationships between God, people, place, and things, the heart must also be involved. *Orthopathos* links orthodoxy and orthopraxis by maximizing emotional acumen to direct *all* of life's experiences to God.[39] *Orthopathos* is the route prescribed by Christ. He transcended the divine realm to enter the arena of human pathos. He then offered the fellowship of the Spirit so that persons can likewise be for one another. *Orthopathos* takes into account Christ's empowering Spirit in people's lives, which presents suffering as a pathway to fullness in God.[40] The Spirit does not lead away from pain but journeys with afflictions to meet joy. And joy, according to theologian Jürgen Moltmann, comprises the Spirit's power "to live, to love, to have creative initiative."[41] Unlike the theoretical model that directly links possessing the right doctrinal system to rouse Christian practices, *orthopathos* considers real-life experiences. It takes the transforming power of the Spirit found at the site of human experiences to hinge together orthodoxy–orthopraxis. This includes instances of joy essential to combatting injustice.

JOY

When it comes to the question of the ways Christians can cultivate an *orthopathos* of joy, Jennings advocates following those who have "learned to ride the winds of chaos." This means entering places belonging to the marginalized who perform home-making creativity to *subravivir* (survive). Latinx, Asian, and Black American survival necessitates gathering spots, communal affairs, collaborative creativity, and play to nourish joy as a method to fight ongoing and accumulating traumas. Like Gates's Stony Island Arts Bank in Grand Crossings, Jennings assumes that joy is the "currency" that flows "between hands."[42] All the more reason why theology and artistic production from the margins are invaluable.

The invitation to probe the geographies of joy further authorizes this exploration of Theaster Gates's investment in urban Black places. His home making highlights a Black American ethos of joy, which, according to Jennings, makes "productive use of pain and suffering."[43] Answering the question of what animates the hope that propagates his investiture of time, money, and gifts toward reactivating materials, people, buildings, and neighborhoods, Gates responds that hope is not the initial force. Instead, it is about accomplishing the task at hand. Without the joy of labor, hope "could burn you out."[44] This sentiment correlates to Jennings's application of joy, where it "becomes a state and a way of life" that continually resists "all the forces of despair."[45] Seen in this light, Gates's vocation as a monk makes sense. His pursuits are not built on hope, though it may be resident. Instead, a monk creates the conditions for others to experience abiding moments, which encompass joy. "You work on the thing in front of you, and then you move on to the next thing," explains Gates.[46] This liberating labor produces a more bountiful development than just hope, yet simultaneously defies hopelessness through joy.

In a society that has drifted from the moorings of communal abiding experiences yet still needs them, Gates's art aims to nourish and reconcile hungry souls. His spiritual vocation in the world brings to light the sacredness of the secular, much like Jennings's locations for "profound realities of indirection."[47] The artist's poetic efforts offer an oblique *kerygma* where "public rituals" that are "bound to real space" provide the type of joy akin to barbershops and beauty salons in Black American neighborhoods.[48] Joy resists the sting of death, holding fast to what brings life, and thus is the spiritual mark of sacrificial hospitality that bears affinities to Christ's incarnational migration through *kenosis*. Gates's art exposes the way sweat, suffering, and the Spirit of God create a kind of "holy ghost" experience in a world where "All we have is brunch . . . in the absence of the temple, art is all we got."[49]

To close, Gates provides a question important for God's image-bearing hosts to consider. "Is it possible to stay in a place and demonstrate a transformation in the quality of life by simply being artful in that place?"[50] Perhaps the song Gates sings at the end of the day provides his answer.

Guide my hands.
Guide my hands.
Guide my hands.
Guide my hands, while I am on this tedious journey.
Guide my hands.[51]

This is the prayer of a theology of hospitality that looks to mirror God's creativity by performing abiding care, reconciling redemption and life-giving endeavors for the sake of joy.

Lift up your heads, O gates! and be lifted up,
O ancient doors! that the King of Glory may come in.
—Psalm 24:7 (NRSV)

Acknowledgments

Initially what drew me to the artist Theaster Gates is the way he addresses property renovation as a social-aesthetic venture. He does so with nonconforming passion to transmit patterns of redemption for the public to see. While the reclamation of city streets lured me in, studying his deeds and declarations opened the door to a holistic perspective previously underrated in the discourses I have been trained in—art and theology, respectively. Gates's invitation to speculate darkly, to enter Black life, not only enlarges my worldview but provides pathways to address and name unformulated items experienced as a woman, Cuban American, artist, religious leader, and scholar in predominately white, male spaces.

As I explore the landscape of Black American life and spirituality, I acknowledge I am but a guest. As an outsider, I can only draw out partial understandings of its complex, rich histories and cultures. I am indebted to the generous hospitality of artists and scholars who became my guides. I learned so much; *docta ignorantia*. For so long, I have neglected the wisdom and wonder of my own heritage. Through the gospel of Theaster Gates and others, I am inspired to finally ponder *latinamente*. It's about time.

I would like to express my profound appreciation to Dr. William Dyrness. As advisor for this project, his enthusiasm enabled a creative freedom to explore art for theology's sake. For the readers' sake, credit goes to Dr. Todd Johnson, who thankfully provided perimeters to the creative chaos that ensued. Thank you, both, for your belief in the subject matter, its method of delivery, and me. I am also honored by the attention given to this project by Dr. Dwight Hopkins.

I am grateful for all past and present colleagues at the Brehm Center, Fuller Seminary, especially Shannon Sigler and Makoto Fujimura. Mako, thank you for allowing me to research, write, and create art in the Brehm/Fujimura Studio. This is truly an important lesson on hospitality. I have been blessed and enlarged by friends at the seminary, bound together by a belief in Christ and the Spirit at work in the world. They have been thought partners, collaborators, mentors, and have offered sweet encouragement and consolation. This includes the Fujimura Fellows and former Theology and Art Capstone students, who are doing the true work of theology and art integration within the current sea change.

Editorial-wise, thank you to Dr. Kutter Callaway, for taking on this project as editor for the Engagement with Culture series; to Brian Fee, for reading several versions of the text; and to Susan Wood—your work on the original manuscript was one of your last labors, and I hope you are honored by this publication. I am flattered by the diligence of Will Bergkamp and Bethany Dickerson at Fortress Press.

Closer to home, I am grateful for Jeannette Scholer. As gracious host, you truly embody Christ's hospitality. I hope to be more like you. Edward and Rochelle Bates, First Presbyterian Church of Hollywood people, thank you for your support during the many years of doctoral studies. Fee clan, you rock. Walker Fee, thanks for collaborating on this project by supplying the wonderful ink illustrations. Finally, my immediate family deserves more than my gratitude. Walker, Maia and Simon, Emma, be blessed. God dwells with you despite the severe alienations of our time. I know you feel them deeply. My dearest Brian, your heart has given me a dwelling place. Thanks for enduring the rocky California years.

Notes

PREFACE

1 I use the term "re-associate" because, prior to the modern era, the arts were an integral part of life together. This is still true in many communities. Scholars Georgina Born, Eric Lewis, and Will Straw relate that there is a need to address the social dimensions of art, noting the ways it fashions the imagination and communicates the drama and ethos of communities. Georgina Born, Eric Lewis, and Will Straw, eds., *Improvisation and Social Aesthetics* (Durham, NC: Duke University Press, 2017), 3.

2 Gesa Elsbeth Thiessen, ed., *Theological Aesthetics: A Reader* (Grand Rapids, MI: Eerdmans, 2004), 11.

3 Theologian Kathryn Reklis makes the salient point that people classified as *other* are particularly sensitive to issues concerning embodiment because they are not recognized in a world where universalizing norms are established by privileged, white, Western males. Kathryn Reklis, *Theology and the Kinesthetic Imagination: Jonathan Edwards and the Making of Modernity* (Oxford: Oxford University Press, 2014), 6.

4 Alexander Schmemann, *For the Life of The World* (Crestwood, NY: St. Vladimir's Seminary Press, 1963), 26–27.

5 The terms "West" or "Western" in this study refer to assessments of the world defined by the history of a male-oriented, European-based, and white perspective. This worldview prefers to construct history temporally, not spatially; it favors the mind/will/rationality as the core of being human. Other knowledge systems (spiritual, intuitive, emotional, physical senses and experiences) are considered suspect. Another emphasis of the West, and modernity, is the notion of autonomy, which undercuts the reality that human formation is established through various relationships with place, people, and things. This diminishes the wisdom and authority of a tribal/clan ethos notable in non-Western societies. A delineation of Western biases will continue throughout this study.

CHAPTER 1

1 Theaster Gates, "Yamaguchi Soul Manufacturing Corporation and a Potter Named Dave," Keynote Lecture, NCECA Conference, Milwaukee, Wisconsin, 2014, accessed August 16, 2022, https://www.youtube.com/watch?v=v_QfJGPP974.

2 John Inge provides the basic definitions for place and space that I adopt here. *Place* refers to the particular, as in locality, while *space* is seen as general, infinite, and abstract. While I have adopted these meanings, quoted persons may use the terms interchangeably. John Inge, *A Christian Theology of Place* (Aldershot, UK: Ashgate, 2003), 1.

3 Michel de Certeau, *The Practice of Everyday Life* (Berkeley: University of California Press, 1984), 98.

4 De Certeau, *The Practice of Everyday Life*, 98. Lisa Yun Lee writes of the influence of de Certeau on Gates. The artist's procedures are *tactics*, subversive gestures that push the boundaries of power system's *strategies* that either give or deny life's gestures their meaning; Lisa Yun Lee, "Survey," in Carol Becker, Lisa Yun Lee, and Achim Borchardt-Hume, *Theaster Gates* (London: Phaidon Press, 2015), 93.

5 From here on, I will refer to the location as Grand Crossings.

6 The installation was entitled *12 Ballads for Huguenot House*, and was exhibited in Kassel's 2012 international art fair. Gates sent sections of 6901 S. Dorchester Avenue to Kassel and arranged them in an abandoned building that once housed Huguenot refugees. Gates and his Chicago crew resided in the Huguenot House in order to play host to art fair visitors.

7 Thanks go to Kate Hadley Toftness, for setting up the guided tour and sharing Dorchester Project stories.

8 Jian Ghomeshi, "The Best of Q: Theaster Gates on the Art of Urban Space," CBC Radio, April 24, 2014, accessed August 16, 2022, https://www.cbc.ca/radio/q/schedule-for-thursday-april-24-1.2983113/best-of-q-theaster-gates-on-the-art-of-urban-space-1.2983357. In regard to the "outmigration" of the Black middle class from the ghetto, see William Julius Wilson, *When Work Disappears* (New York: Vintage, 1996), 46.

9 Rebuild Foundation, "Mission Statement," accessed March 22, 2016, https://rebuild-foundation.org/about/our-story/. Rebuild Foundation's mission is to reconstruct "the cultural foundations" of "underinvested" communities. From here on, Rebuild Foundation will be identified simply as Rebuild.

10 Diana Nawi, "Interview with Theaster Gates," *Art Practical*, November 14, 2012, accessed September 26, 2022, https://wayback.archive-it.org/15633/20210126063032/https://www.artpractical.com/feature/interview_with_theaster_gates/.

11 This performance-based or multidiscipline art genre aimed to move art from being object-oriented to conceptually based. It looked to redefine art by loosening art/life distinctions through performances or event-based methods.

12 Rebecca Zorach, "Art & Soul: An Experimental Friendship between the Street and a Museum," *Art Journal* 70, no. 2 (Summer 2011): 80–81. In a footnote, the author mentions Gates's support of her research that highlights Chicago's historical Black art endeavors, which are barely mentioned in the cannon of Western art history.

13 Josef Sorett, *Spirit in the Dark: A Religious History of Racial Aesthetics* (New York: Oxford University Press, 2016), 156. Sorett relates that the movement offered an aesthetic rooted in lived experiences as a way to validate Black identity.

14 Melissa Harris, "Artist Banks on Cultural Payback," *Chicago Tribune*, August 5, 2012.

15 John Colapinto, "The Real-Estate Artist," *The New Yorker*, January 20, 2014, 26.

16 Rachel Furnari, "High Spirits: The Artist Theaster Gates Can't Stop Reaching New Heights," *NewCity Art*, March 30, 2010, accessed August 16, 2022, http://art.newcity.com/2010/03/30/high-spirits-artist -theaster-gates-cant-stop-reaching-new-heights/.

17 Colapinto, "The Real-Estate Artist," 26.

18 Theaster Gates, "Theaster Gates in 'Chicago,'" Season 8, Art21, September 2016, accessed August 16, 2022, https://art21.org/watch/art-in-the-twenty -first-century/s8/theaster-gates-in-chicago-segment/.

19 Diane Solway, "The Change Agent," *W* 42, no. 6 (June 2013): 96. In a replay of his artistic career, Gates also shares that one of his first social work jobs was to build an afterschool program for a Christian organization using ceramics as a means to provide care for indigent teenage Native Americans in the Seattle area. Theaster Gates, "Artist Talk—But to Be a Poor Race," Conversation with Theaster Gates and Hamza Walker, Regen Projects, Los Angeles, January 15, 2017.

20 This form of art is also known as social aesthetics, or socially engaged art. Acknowledging that aesthetic experiences hold social implications, artists employ multiple art disciplines and social discourses toward addressing social concerns.

21 The Artes Mundi 6 prize (2015), Nasher Prize Laureate (2018), and Vision of the City artist grant (2019) are just a few of the art-world honors Theaster Gates holds.

22 Nato Thompson, *Living as Form: Socially Engaged Art from 1991–2011* (New York: MIT Press, 2012), 21.

23 Theaster Gates, "Artist Talk."

24 Jeffrey Deitch, "Jeffrey Deitch & Theaster Gates: I Believe in Places," The Avant/Garde Diaries, Mercedes-Benz, January 13, 2012, YouTube video, 4:13, accessed August 16, 2022, https://www.youtube.com/watch?v=m34aIZG-_JM.

25 This method follows the example given by the French philosopher Gaston Bachelard in *The Poetics of Space: The Classic Look at How We Experience Intimate Places,* trans. Maria Jolas (Boston: Beacon Press, 1994, repr. ed.), 38. Here, he reads the houses and rooms depicted in literary pages as a means to exegete the psychological logic of its authors, thus determining their affections.

26 Richard McCoy, "Exploring the Freedom to Re-Present Value: A Discussion with Theaster Gates," *Art21 Magazine,* April 19, 2011, accessed August 16, 2022, http://magazine.art21.org/2011/04/19/no-preservatives-exploring-the-freedom-to-re-present-value-a-discussion-with-theaster-gates/#.Yvt153bMJPY.

27 One example of this type of educational opportunity hosted at Dorchester Art + Housing Collaborative through Rebuild is Project Tool. Rebuild Dancer-in-Residence Onye Ozuzu combined building tools experiences with dance to link both kinds of labors and further align mind–body connections. Rebuild Foundation E-Newsletter, week of September 4, 2017.

28 Miwon Kwon, *One Place after Another: Site-Specific Art and Locality Identity* (Cambridge, MA: MIT Press, 2004), 8.

29 John Owens, "Shuttered CHA Complex Gets New Life as Artists' Home," *Chicago Tribune,* November 11, 2014, accessed August 16, 2022, http://www.chicagotribune.com/news/local/ct-dorchester-collaborative-met-20141111-story.html.

30 Colapinto, "The Real-Estate Artist," 24–31.

31 Simone Weil, *Waiting for God* (New York: Harper Torchbooks, 1973), 139. Weil states that the gospel "makes no distinctions between the love of neighbor and justice." For Weil, grace is felt in three particular forms that are also found in Gates's work: religious ceremonies, beauty, and care of neighbor (137–38). Also, see Elaine Scarry, *On Beauty and Being Just* (Princeton, NJ: Princeton University Press, 1999).

32 Christine D. Pohl, *Making Room: Recovering Hospitality as a Christian Tradition* (Grand Rapids, MI: Eerdmans, 1999), 10.

33 Thank you, Anansi kNowBody and Maya Lori, for your time, warmth, and open hospitality.

34 While artists have creatively repurposed and salvaged materials since Picasso and Braque's collages (1912), the term "upcycling" originates as a design term regarding manufacturing elements that reduce waste and environmental issues explored by architect William McDonough and scientist Michael Braungart in their book *Cradle to Cradle: Remaking the Way We Make Things* (New York: North Point Press, 2002).

35 "I see the bank as an object that has been resurrected. I think the things in the bank demonstrate . . . whatever we have, it gives life to other things," explains Gates. Theaster Gates, "Working the Public, with Theaster Gates," interview by Naima J. Keith, California African American Museum, Los Angeles, January 24, 2018.

36 Lily Wei, "In the Studio: Theaster Gates," *Art in America* 99, no. 11 (December 2011): 125.

37 Carol Becker, "Interview," in Carol Becker, Lisa Yun Lee, and Achim Borchardt-Hume, *Theaster Gates* (London: Phaidon, 2015), 28–31. Unlike Duchamp's famous readymade urinal, the marble urinal stall was handled and thus leverages the labor or the somatic filtration phase of Gates's circular ecology.

38 Theaster Gates, "Visual Thoughts," in *Theaster Gates: 12 Ballads for Huguenot House*, dOCUMENTA 13, by Michael Darling et al. (Cologne: Walther Konig, 2012), 26.

39 Edward W. Soja, *Postmodern Geographies: The Reassertion of Space in Critical Social Theory*, 2nd ed. (London: Verso, 1989), 134.

40 Fred Moten, "Nowhere, Everywhere," in *Theaster Gates: My Labor Is My Protest*, ed. Honey Luard (London: White Cube Gallery, 2013), 76. "Gates sounds an epitaph for that desire in alternative longing that loudly keeps its own apostolic counsel," effuses Moten.

41 "The call to arms that my work is suggesting," says Gates, "is that there are different ways of establishing value, and that money is not the only way"; McCoy, "Exploring the Freedom to Re-Present Value."

42 Michael Wright, "An Aesthetic of Contemplative Art-Making," conference lecture, Christians in the Visual Arts, Azusa Pacific University, Azusa, CA, June 17, 2017.

43 Richard Harper, at the conference "Theaster Gates: A Way of Working," Vera List Prize for Art and Politics, The New School, New York, September 18, 2013, accessed August 22, 2022, http://www.veralistcenter.org/engage/event/1885/theaster-gates-a-way-of-working/.

44 Radhika Subramanian, at the conference "Theaster Gates: A Way of Working," Vera List Prize for Art and Politics, The New School, New York, September 18, 2013, accessed August 22, 2022, http://www.veralistcenter.org/engage/event/1885/theaster-gates-a-way-of-working/.

45 In Gates's piece entitled *Migration Rickshaw for Sleeping, Building, and Playing*, a rolled-up mattress is tethered atop a pile of timeworn housing lumber stacked on a makeshift cart with wheels. The side panels are stair stringers, alluding to the deconstruction/possible future reconstruction of home.

46 Examples of Gates's material migration include the use of floorboards from Wrigley Gum factory that furnished Gates's structure in *Temple Exercises*

(2009) and the gathering of decommissioned fire hoses that fashion Gates's Civil Rights Tapestries.

47 Moten, "Nowhere, Everywhere," 70.

48 Moten's claim resonates with the philosopher Walter Benjamin's historical materialist view, which defends the idea that images belonging to the oppressed past must be recognized "in order to blast a specific life out of the era or a specific work out of the lifework"; Walter Benjamin, "Theses on the Philosophy of History," in *Illuminations* (New York: Schocken Books, 2007), section 17, 262. Benjamin indicates that the present carries unfulfilled yearnings for an earlier period's anticipated fruits never acquired. The remedy for such unrequited hopes is awareness of the future and how it is "indissolubly bound up with the image of redemption" that must deal with such past discontinuities (254). Benjamin contends that if the disparities of the past are not acknowledged by the present, the past will "disappear irretrievably" (255). Likewise, Gates discloses that he is "interested in reconstructing histories and intervening in futures," echoing Benjamin's thought; Wei, "In the Studio: Theaster Gates," 126.

49 Kwon, *One Place after Another*, 2–3.

50 Mitchell Duneier, *Ghetto: The Invention of a Place, the History of an Idea* (New York: Farrar, Straus & Giroux, 2016), 29–30.

51 Soja, *Postmodern Geographies*, 35.

52 Gates uses the term *leverage* to designate the active critical role the arts play in calling attention to issues. Yet the artist also actually advances place, people, and things through his redemptive artistic programs.

53 Pohl, *Making Room*, 174.

54 John Colapinto notes that Gates read about Lowe and connected the Texan artist's place-based interventions with the teachings of Sam Mockbee, about whom Gates learned at Iowa State. Gates further sought out Lowe and invited him to Grand Crossings ("The Real-Estate Artist," 29). See also Lisa Yun Lee, "Everything and the Burden Is Beautiful," in Carol Becker, Lisa Yun Lee, and Achim Borchardt-Hume, *Theaster Gates* (London: Phaidon, 2015), 52.

55 Tom Finkelpearl, "Interview: Rick Lowe on Designing Project Row Houses," in *Dialogues in Public Art*, ed. Tom Finkelpearl and Vito Acconci (Cambridge, MA: MIT Press, 2000), 268.

56 W. E. B. DuBois, *The Souls of Black Folk* (New York: Dover Publications, 1994), 2. "BETWEEN ME AND THE OTHER WORLD there is ever an unmasked question." The question works as a "vast veil" from the white world, where opportunities "were theirs, not mine."

57 The word "liturgy" refers to (1) Christian worship rituals of and for the people of God, and (2) its original meaning *leiturgia*, which describes patrons' works to benefit the public, thus encompassing cultural endeavors.

In fact, I am arguing that the liturgies of the church can shape and rouse secular liturgies.

58 Walter Brueggemann, *The Land: Place as Gift, Promise, and Challenge in Biblical Faith*, 2nd ed. (Minneapolis: Fortress, 2002), 178.

59 I extend thanks to Todd Johnson for this insight.

60 Ellen Davis, *Scripture, Culture, and Agriculture: An Agrarian Reading of the Bible* (New York: Cambridge University Press, 2009), 15.

61 Sorett, *Spirit in the Dark*, 217.

62 For the theologian James Cone, God's divine liberation, exemplified in the life of Christ, is the ground for justice, the care of others. "Because of Jesus Christ, our behavior can now be defined by divine behavior"; James Cone, *God of the Oppressed* (Maryknoll, NY: Orbis, 1997), 189.

63 Sorett, *Spirit in the Dark*, 216.

64 John Perkins, *Beyond Charity* (Grand Rapids, MI: Baker Books, 1993), 127. Perkins initiated the Christian Community Development Association to help faith-based communities construct their own community improvement infrastructures and operations. While evangelicals look to Perkins as a model, it must be noted that segments of the Black church have long practiced custodial stewardship with an entrepreneurial spirit. My thanks go to community development activist and pastor Delonte Gholston for this insight.

65 Theaster Gates, "Changing Chicago One Block at a Time: Theaster Gates," interview, Windy City Live, May 2, 2016, Chicago: ABC/WLS-TV, accessed August 22, 2022, http://abc7chicago.com/society/changing-chicago-one-block-at-a-time-theaster-gates/1318611/.

66 C. Eric Lincoln and Lawrence Mamiya, *The Black Church in the African American Experience* (Durham, NC: Duke University Press, 1990), 273. For a history of African American ethical economic cooperatives, see Jessica Gordon Nembhard, *Collective Courage: A History of African American Cooperative Economic Thought and Practice* (University Park: Pennsylvania State University Press, 2014).

67 Lincoln and Mamiya, *The Black Church in the African American Experience*, 9.

68 Lincoln and Mamiya, 2.

69 Theaster Gates, "Yamaguchi Soul Manufacturing Corporation and a Potter Named Dave," Keynote Lecture, NCECA Conference, Milwaukee, Wisconsin, 2014, accessed August 22, 2022, https://www.youtube.com/watch?v=v_QfJGPP974.

70 Flora Wilson Bridges, *Resurrection Song: African American Spirituality* (Maryknoll, NY: Orbis, 2001), 3.

71 Biography notes from "Theaster Gates," Artsy, accessed November 24, 2020, https://www.artsy.net/artist/theaster-gates.

72 Wilson Bridges, *Resurrection Song*, 16.

73 On the notion of spirituality as a characteristic of a Black American worldview, see: W. E. B. Du Bois, "The Genius of the Negro Church," in *The Souls of Black Folk*, 120; Lincoln and Mamiya, *The Black Church in the African American Experience*, 338; Estrelda Alexander, *Black Fire: One Hundred Years of African American Pentecostalism* (Downers Grove, IL: IVP Academic, 2011), 16.

74 This is Max Weber's term, phrased at the onset of the twentieth century to denote the enterprising nature of Protestants. He observed the way their faith formation seemed to be fulfilled through secular activity (29). He also claimed that Calvinism shared an "inner affinity" with "modern capital culture" (7); Max Weber, *The Protestant Ethic and the Spirit of Capitalism* (New York: Penguin Classics, 2002).

75 Cone, *God of the Oppressed*, 224.

76 Cone, 127. According to Cone, Jesus Christ is the experienced "Word of liberation" that empowers the "struggle for freedom" because, as the theologian reveals, "God is struggling too" (178).

77 Catherine Pickstock, "Liturgy, Art, and Politics," *Modern Theology* 16, no. 2 (April 2000): 179.

CHAPTER 2

1 Carol Becker, "Interview," in Carol Becker, Lisa Yun Lee, and Achim Borchardt-Hume, *Theaster Gates* (London: Phaidon, 2015), 8.

2 Leonard Todd, "Carolina Clay: The Life and Legend of the Slave Potter, Dave," Leonardtod.com, accessed April 3, 2017, http://leonardtodd.com /daves-poems_284.html.

3 Gates's shared enterprise with Kohler's white workers invited them to "speculate darkly" about Dave. Their labor became the common denominator.

4 In collaboration with the musician Leroy Bach of Wilco fame, Gates published the music as *My Name Is Dave: A Hymnal*; Lisa Yun Lee, "Survey," in Carol Becker, Lisa Yun Lee, and Achim Borchardt-Hume, *Theaster Gates* (London: Phaidon, 2015), 86.

5 Anthony Pinn and Benjamin Valentin, "Introduction," in *Ties That Bind: African American and Hispanic/Latino/a Theologies in Dialogue*, ed. Anthony Pinn and Benjamin Valentin (New York: Continuum, 2001), 48.

6 Pinn and Valentin, "Introduction," in *Ties That Bind*, 13.

7 Becker, "Interview," 8.

8 Karl Rahner, *Theological Investigations*, vol. 4: *More Recent Writings* (Baltimore: Helicon Press, 1966), 224.

9 Rahner, *Theological Investigations*, 4:229.

10 Rahner, *Theological Investigations*, 4:225.

11 W. E. B. Du Bois, *The Souls of Black Folk* (New York: Dover Publications, 1994), 2. Du Bois's "double consciousness" entails consideration of the Black self through the comparison lens of white normativity: "A world which yields him no true self-consciousness, but only lets him see himself through the revelation of the other world."

12 Rahner, *Theological Investigations*, 4:229–30.

13 According to James Cone, "It is called *survival* because it is a way of remaining physically alive in a situation of oppression without losing one's dignity"; James Cone, *Black Theology and Black Power*, 20th anniversary ed. (San Francisco: HarperSanFrancisco, 1989), 2.

14 Soyini Madison, Foreword to Thomas F. DeFrantz and Anita Gonzalez, eds., *Black Performance Theory* (Durham, NC: Duke University Press, 2014), vii–ix. See also DuBois, *The Souls of Black Folk*, 123.

15 Rahner, *Theological Investigations*, 4:230–31.

16 This idea of monumental place derives from the spatial theorist Henri Lefebvre's idea of bodies. The public-facing facet of a body or bodies creates a *property* representing the ethos of body/bodies along with "the status of 'subjects.'" Thus, bodies become a "monumental space"; Henri Lefebvre, *The Production of Space* (Oxford: Blackwell, 1991), 224.

17 Carl Paris, "Reading the 'Spirit' and the Dancing Body in the Choreography of Ronald K. Brown and Reggie Wilson," in *Black Performance Theory*, ed. DeFrantz and Gonzalez, 103, 113.

18 Huey Copeland, "Unfinished Business as Usual: African American Artists, New York Museums, and the 1990s," in *Come as You Are: Art of the 1990s*, ed. Alexandra Schwartz (Oakland: University of California Press, 2015), 31–32.

19 Eric Garner, Michael Brown, Tamir Rice, Ataliana Jefferson, Stephon Clark, Philando Castille, George Floyd, Breonna Taylor, and Ahmaud Arbery to name just a portion from a long list of victims of law-enforcement brutalities.

20 "We Broke Down ArtReview's Power 100 by Race, Gender, Profession, and Place of Birth," *Artsy*, October 19, 2016, accessed August 22, 2022, https://www.artsy.net/article/artsy-editorial-we-broke-down-the-art-world-s-100-most-powerful-people-by-race-gender-profession-and-place-of-birth; "We Broke Down ArtReview's Power 100 by Race, Gender, Profession, and Place of Birth," *Artsy*, November 2, 2017, accessed August 22, 2022, https://www.artsy.net/article/artsy-editorial-broke-artreviews-power-100-race-gender-profession-place-birth; ArtReview, Power 100, 2019, accessed August 22, 2022, https://artreview.com/power-100?year=2019.

21 "Theaster Gates, Talk at Armory 2011," January 7, 2011, YouTube video, accessed August 22, 2022, https://www.youtube.com/watch?v=V6dDKYAqt8o.

22 Theaster Gates, "Yamaguchi Soul Manufacturing Corporation and a Potter Named Dave," Keynote Lecture, NCECA Conference, Milwaukee, WI, September 23, 2014, https://www.youtube.com/watch?v=v_QfJGPP974.

23 "Theaster Gates and Carolyn Christov-Bakargiev in Conversation," in *Theaster Gates: 12 Ballads for Huguenot House*, dOCUMENTA 13, by Michael Darling et al. (Cologne: Walther Konig, 2012), 15.

24 Regarding the trickster motif, see William Courtland Johnson, "Trickster on Trial: The Morality of the Brer Rabbit Tales," in *"Ain't Gonna Lay My 'Ligion Down": African American Religion in the South*, ed. Alonzo Johnson and Paul Jersild (Columbia: University of South Carolina Press, 1996), 59. Also, Daphne Brooks, *Bodies in Dissent: Spectacular Performances of Race and Freedom, 1850–1910* (Durham, NC: Duke University Press, 2006), 2.

25 Jennifer A. González, "Costume: Come as You Aren't," in *Come as You Are: Art of the 1990s*, ed. Alexandra Schwartz (Oakland: University of California Press, 2015), 37.

26 Fred Wilson's 1991 *Guarded View* similarly speaks of the obscurity of minorities in art spaces. The piece consists of four dark-skinned mannequins dressed in the security guard uniforms that represent New York City museums. It is significant to mention that the figures are headless.

27 An earlier performance of absence relevant to both Gates and Wilson is Mierle Laderman Ukeles's 1973 mopping of museum floors. Through the act, she referred to an unappreciated museum maintenance staff, as well as the void of exhibiting women's art. Forty years later, Ukeles's swapping movement is echoed in Gates's application of tar on objects to honor his father's maintenance trade as a roofer.

28 For Gates, there is "beauty inside that poverty that is Black power"; Theaster Gates, "Artist Talk: Theaster Gates—But to Be a Poor Race," conversation with Hamza Walker, Regen Projects, Los Angeles, January 15, 2017. Gates's comment corresponds with theologian James Cone's concept of Black power, which is the ability to self-affirm amid negations; Cone, *Black Theology and Black Power*, 60. According to Gates, this power is also spiritual: "I'm not interested and occupied with Black power. Not Black Panther power—but Black spiritual and religious power," notes Gates; Carolina Miranda, "Artist Theaster Gates on W. E. B. DuBois and What Donald Trump Doesn't Get about Chicago," *Los Angeles Times*, January 27, 2017, accessed August 22, 2022, http://www.latimes.com/entertainment/arts/miranda/la-et-cam-theaster-gates-regen-projects-20170127-story.html.

29 In the Black American and African diasporic context, the spiritual encompasses a wide variety of meanings that give merit to unseen forces, such

as divinity, God, soul agency, and life force. Gates's oeuvre exhibits this type of open, deep, yet also ambiguous spirituality and sometimes aligns it with power or a kinesthetic epistemology.

30 Tom McDonough, "Theaster Gates," [interview] *BOMB* 130, Winter 2014–2015, accessed August 22, 2022, http://bombmagazine.org/article/2000073/theaster-gates. Gates can name actual Japanese craft masters, but African cultic performances and their utensils receive little artist recognition. "It's denying the deep intellectual regime that traditional carvers, craftsmen, diviners, and spiritualists had," Gates asserts in the interview with Tom McDonough.

31 This spiritual dimension is congruent with Professor of Religion and African Studies Josef Sorett's exploration of Black secular spirituality of the New Negro era (1920s) and the Black Arts movement (1960s and 1970s). Sorett denotes the way these respective generations of Black intellectuals utilized a "grammar of spirit" to reflect and resolve the constraints of the Black American context, which also operated as a mark of Afro distinction. Josef Sorett, *Spirit in The Dark: A Religious History of Racial Aesthetics* (New York: Oxford University Press, 2016), 8–9.

32 Willie James Jennings, *The Christian Imagination: Theology and the Origins of Race* (New Haven, CT: Yale University Press, 2010), 16.

33 McDonough, "Theaster Gates."

34 My thanks go to Dr. Dwight Hopkins for providing this outline; Dwight Hopkins, *Being Human: Race, Culture, and Religion* (Minneapolis: Fortress, 2005), 160–61.

35 Gerhard von Rad, *Old Testament Theology*, vol. 2 (Edinburgh: Oliver & Boyd, 1965), 338–39.

36 Old Testament scholar Catherine McDowell presents four historical and standard readings of *imago Dei*: (1) McDowell maintains that throughout the ages, many have speculated that humanity's mental, spiritual, reasoning, and moral faculties constitute icon status (Philo, Luther, Calvin). (2) Yet she also makes note of a strain in rabbinical theology that interprets *imago Dei* in the physical sense. (3) Theologians like Barth define image and likeness in regard to humanity's capacity for relationships. For Barth, this is signified by gender differences. As a unified diversity, humanity reflects God's Triune being. (4) Finally, McDowell notes that the dominion/stewardship language that surrounds the premise of *imago Dei* indicates royal ideology (J. Hehn). Humans are meant to represent God in the similar fashion of a king and his corresponding ersatz representatives; Catherine McDowell, "In the Image of God He Created Them," in *Image of God in an Image Driven Age: Explorations in Theological Anthropology*, ed. Beth Felker Jones and Jeffrey Barbeau (Downers Grove, IL: IVP Academic, 2016), 30–34.

37 Richard Lints, *Identity and Idolatry: The Image of God and Its Inversion* (Downers Grove, IL: InterVarsity Press, 2015), 153.

38 Lints, *Identity and Idolatry*, 21–23.

39 See Catherine McDowell, *The Image of God in the Garden of Eden* (Winona Lake, IN: Eisenbrauns, 2015), 106–7.

40 Theaster Gates, "Working the Public, with Theaster Gates," interview by Naima J. Keith, California African American Museum, Los Angeles, January 24, 2018.

41 Michelle Wright, *Becoming Black* (Durham, NC: Duke University Press, 2004), 64.

42 Willie James Jennings, "Aesthetic Struggle and Ecclesial Vision," in *Black Practical Theology*, ed. Dale B. Andrews and Robert London Smith Jr. (Waco: Baylor University Press, 2015), 163.

43 Jennings, "Aesthetic Struggle and Ecclesial Vision," 174.

44 Jennings, "Aesthetic Struggle and Ecclesial Vision," 170–71.

45 Willie James Jennings, *The Christian Imagination: Theology and the Origins of Race* (New Haven, CT: Yale University Press, 2010), 6.

46 It takes the empathic agency of those who are triple marginalized to originate and actuate such a movement; Alicia Garza, Patrisse Cullors, and Ayọ (formerly Opal) Tometi are Black, female, and queer.

47 Luis Pedraja, "Building Bridges between Communities of Struggle: Similarities, Differences, Objectives, and Goals," in *Ties That Bind*, ed. Pinn and Valentin, 217–18.

48 Lints, *Identity and Idolatry*, 76.

49 Jennings, "Aesthetic Struggle and Ecclesial Vision," 174.

50 St. John of Damascus, *Three Treatises on the Divine Images*, trans. Andrew Louth (Crestwood, NY: St. Vladimir's Seminary Press, 2003), 109. St. John further writes, "For what reason, then, do we adore one another, except because we have been made to the image of God?"; John of Damascus, "From *Orthodox Faith*," in *Theological Aesthetics: A Reader*, ed. Gesa Elsbeth Thiessen (Grand Rapids, MI: Eerdmans, 2004), 68.

51 John of Damascus, *Three Treatises on the Divine Images*, 107.

52 Gates, "Working the Public."

53 Jennings, "Aesthetic Struggle and Ecclesial Vision," 163.

54 Jennings, "Aesthetic Struggle and Ecclesial Vision," 164–65.

55 Jennings, "Aesthetic Struggle and Ecclesial Vision," 182.

56 Miroslav Volf, *Exclusion and Embrace: A Theological Exploration of Identity, Otherness, and Reconciliation* (Nashville: Abingdon, 1996), 49–50.

57 For instance, theologian Dwight Hopkins considers the way "selves," a community, shape "the self"; Hopkins, *Being Human*, 4.

58 Lints, *Identity and Idolatry*, 63.

59 Lints, *Identity and Idolatry*, 120

60 Jennings, "Aesthetic Struggle and Ecclesial Vision," 181.

61 Lints, *Identity and Idolatry,* 70.

62 Hopkins, *Being Human,* 160–61.

63 Becker, "Interview," 8.

CHAPTER 3

1 Kelly Huang, "An Artist and a Citizen," *ART21 Magazine* (blog), October 30, 2009, accessed August 22, 2022, http://blog.art21.org/2009/10/30/an-artist-and-a-citizen/.

2 As part of the museum's initiative to extend hospitality, curator Stephanie Smith examined the various meanings artists "sparked" as they redeployed the quotidian task of meal sharing with others. Subsequently, director Anthony Hirschel commented on the "vitality" that filled the museum's galleries as artist-led meals prompted "interactions between artists, visitors, visitors and staff, staff and artists." It was noted that that "living spirit of radical hospitality broke down barriers"; Stephanie Smith, ed., *Feast: Radical Hospitality in Contemporary Art* (Chicago: Smart Museum of Art, University of Chicago, 2013), 8.

3 Gaston Bachelard, *The Poetics of Space: The Classic Look at How We Experience Intimate Places,* trans. Maria Jolas (Boston: Beacon Press, 1994, repr. ed.), 38. Bachelard "reads" the houses and rooms depicted in literary pages as a means to exegete "psychological diagrams" of its authors to offer an "analysis of intimacy."

4 Neil Cummings, "Reading Things: The Alibi of Use," in *Sight Works: Reading Things v. 3,* ed. Neil Cummings (London: Chance Books, 1993), 14. Here, Cumming relates that material objects "trap historically transient experiences."

5 Matthew Jesse Jackson, "The Emperor of the Post-Medium Condition," in *Theaster Gates: 12 Ballads for Huguenot House*, dOCUMENTA 13, by Michael Darling et al. (Cologne: Walther Konig, 2012), 19.

6 Theaster Gates, "Theaster Gates: Soul Food Pavilion," Smart Museum of Art, February 24, 2012, Vimeo, accessed August 22, 2022, http://vimeo.com/37407879.

7 bell hooks, *Yearning: Race, Gender, and Cultural Politics* (Boston: South End Press, 1990), 42.

8 Gates, "Theaster Gates: Soul Food Pavilion."

9 John Howard Yoder, *Body Politics* (Scottdale, PA: Herald Press, 2001), 20.

10 Barbara Holmes, *Joy Unspeakable: Contemplative Practices of the Black Church* (Minneapolis: Augsburg Fortress, 2004), v.

11 Holmes, *Joy Unspeakable,* 14, 15.

12 Huang, "An Artist and a Citizen."

13 Shannon Jackson, *Social Works: Performing Art, Supporting Publics* (New York: Routledge, 2011), 140. Jackson is commenting on the art and writings of Pope.L, who says, "Lack of material is not Lack of immaterial."

14 Jackson, *Social Works*, 135.

15 Theaster Gates, "Working the Public, with Theaster Gates," interview by Naima J. Keith, California African American Museum, Los Angeles, January 24, 2018.

16 Huang, "An Artist and a Citizen." Gates's artistic query regarding rice and its consumers corresponds to the artist Ritkrit Tiravanija's *Untitled 2001 (the magnificent seven, spaghetti western)* where the title alludes to cultural hybridity and communion through the medium of noodles and film. The piece consisted of serving gallery guests Tom Ka Gai from seven vats of soup. The number of soup vats referenced the "good guys" in the film *The Magnificent Seven*; Hannah Higgins, "Schlurrp: The Case for and Against Spaghetti," in Smith, *Feast*, 45.

17 Lily Wei, "In the Studio: Theaster Gates," *Art in America* 99, no. 11 (December 2011): 120–27.

18 Bachelard, *The Poetics of Space*, xxviii.

19 Flora Wilson Bridges, *Resurrection Song: African American Spirituality* (Maryknoll, NY: Orbis, 2001), 165.

20 Gates, "Theaster Gates: Soul Food Pavilion."

21 Jan Verwoert, "The Anti-Angelic Host: Reading the Polities of Hosting Culture through the Writing of Virginia Wolf," in *Feast*, ed. Smith, 361.

22 Miwon Kwon, "The Becoming of a Work of Art: FGT and a Possibility of Renewal, a Chance to Share, a Fragile Truce," in *Felix Gonzalez-Torres*, ed. Julie Ault (New York: Steidldangin, 2016), 286.

23 Gates, "Theaster Gates: Soul Food Pavilion."

24 Diane Solway, "The Change Agent," *W* 42, no. 6 (June 2013): 96.

25 Huang, "An Artist and a Citizen."

26 hooks, *Yearning*, 39.

27 Gates, "Working the Public."

28 Fred Moten, *In the Break: Aesthetics of the Black Radical Tradition* (Minneapolis: University of Minnesota Press, 2003), 26.

29 bell hooks, *All About Love: New Visions* (New York: Harper Perennial, 2001), 83.

30 hooks, *All About Love*, 77.

31 Holmes, *Joy Unspeakable*, 170.

32 Gates, "Working the Public."

33 Regis Duffy, *Real Presence: Worship, Sacraments, and Commitment* (New York: Harper & Row, 1982), 17–19.

34 Duffy, *Real Presence*, 3.

35 Jürgen Moltmann, *The Spirit of Life: A Universal Affirmation* (Minneapolis: Fortress, 2001), 86.

36 Moltmann, *The Spirit of Life*, 17.

37 Concerning his "fix-it" inclination, Gates notes: "I have an appetite for junk. . . . I have an appetite for other people's problems"; Theaster Gates, "The Making of a Con(temporary) Black Public," lecture at UChicago Center in Delhi, December 5, 2017, accessed August 22, 2022, https://www.youtube.com/watch?v=iu_2AtaTgjo&t=76s.

38 Raimundo Panikkar, *Worship and Secular Man* (Maryknoll, NY: Orbis, 1973), 93. Theologian Amos Yong offers more on Panikkar's notion on the vocation of the urban monk through Panikkar's "cosmotheandric" worldview. Within this holistic schema, the world (*cosmos*), divine (*theos*), and human (*anthropos*) agencies work in tandem. Consequently, it becomes the monk's role to enable fuller expressions of humanness by fashioning avenues for transcendence, enabling human fellowship, and revealing the "sacred in and through phenomena"; Amos Yong, *Hospitality and the Other: Pentecost, Christian Practices, and the Neighbor* (Maryknoll, NY: Orbis, 2008), 91.

39 Gates, "Working the Public."

40 Bernard Cooke and Gary Macy, *Christian Symbol and Ritual: An Introduction* (Oxford: Oxford University Press, 2005), 52.

41 Jeffrey Vanderwilt, *A Church without Borders* (Collegeville, MN: Liturgical Press, 1998), 18. Vanderwilt notes that hosting cultivates "the preconditions for communion." Moreover, it is the Holy Spirit's task to change persons at both Christ's table and our own.

42 Michael Skelley, *The Liturgy of the World: Karl Rahner's Theology of Worship* (Collegeville, MN: Liturgical Press, 1991), 75.

43 Paul F. Bradshaw, *The Search for the Origins of Christian Worship* (Oxford: Oxford University Press, 2002), 7.

44 Andrew McGowan, *Ascetic Eucharists: Food and Drink in Early Christian Eucharistic Ritual Meals* (Oxford: Oxford University Press, 1999), 5.

45 Dennis Edwin Smith, *From the Symposium to Eucharist* (Minneapolis: Augsburg Press, 2003), 110.

46 McGowan, *Ascetic Eucharists*, 61.

47 Vanderwilt, *A Church without Borders*, 16.

48 Vanderwilt, *A Church without Borders*, 20.

49 Indeed, the pleasures of *koinōnia*, as well as the format of the Mediterranean banquet-symposium, are echoed in Gates's *Soul Food Pavilion*. For instance, the ethical discussions of the symposium that catalog social mores also find voice at Gates's table. Yet, unlike banquets' social strategies, Gates seats people from a mix of social classes. Perhaps, then, *Soul Food Pavilion* mimics the *koinōnia*, the fellowship ethos of the Black church that invites strangers into their midst as if they were family. Scholars C. Eric Lincoln

and Lawrence Mamiya's study of Black American church and society point to the spiritual uplift afforded by social opportunities in the vein of church dinners and church picnics. And, like the dramatic or musical performances of ancient Near East symposiums, Black churches likewise operated as a theater, concert arena, and art gallery. When church kitchens become the hub of activity, a different kind of care is enacted to nourish participants; C. Eric Lincoln and Lawrence Mamiya, *The Black Church in the African American Experience* (Durham, NC: Duke University Press, 1990), 312.

50 McGowan, *Ascetic Eucharists*, 1.

51 Arthur A. Just Jr., *The Ongoing Feast: Table Fellowship and Eschatology at Emmaus* (Collegeville, MN: Liturgical Press, 1993), 128. This insight supports the premise of a theology of hospitality regarding God's covenantal commitment to care for place, people, and material things.

52 Just, *The Ongoing Feast*, 26.

53 Willi Braun, *Feasting and Social Rhetoric in Luke 14* (New York: Cambridge University Press, 1995), 91.

54 Braun, *Feasting and Social Rhetoric*, 131.

55 Vanderwilt, *A Church without Borders*, 28.

56 My thanks go to Todd Johnson, for this insight that concludes the section.

57 According to New Testament scholar Gordon Fee, Paul understood that when the very visible and tangible food elements were passed across social divisions, they loudly proclaimed both the Lord's death and the unfolding of his kingdom until total fulfillment. Between these two temporal markers, those seated at the table constituted a new people. Gordon Fee, *The First Epistle to the Corinthians*, rev. ed., NICNT (Grand Rapids, MI: Eerdmans, 2014), 469.

58 See Fee, *The First Epistle to the Corinthians*, 617.

59 Mary Jane Jacob, *Grain of Emptiness: Buddhism-Inspired Contemporary Art* (New York: Rubin Museum of Art, 2010), 63.

60 Jürgen Moltmann, *Theology of Joy* (New York: Harper & Row, 1972), 26. Moltmann notes that there is no compelling reason why God would become man. "Yet in his infinite love he is *well-pleased* to do just that."

61 Rowan Williams, "Rights, Recognition, and the Body of Christ," Payton Lectures, Fuller Theological Seminary, Pasadena, CA, April 5, 2018.

62 Williams, "Rights, Recognition, and the Body of Christ."

63 Charles Taylor notes that a collective identity, "whether it be that of a nation, or an ethnic group, or religious movement," cherishes and upholds ideas of the good. "Here is a crucial collective good which seems 'consubstantial' with God, or in some essential relation to transcendence." Furthermore, this "consubstantiality" can be a way "in which the immanent frame may be inherently open to transcendence"; Charles Taylor, *A Secular Age* (Cambridge, MA: Belknap Press, 2007), 545.

64 Gordon Fee, *Paul, the Spirit, and the People of God* (Peabody, MA: Hendrickson, 1996), xv.

65 Holmes, *Joy Unspeakable*, 14. Theologian Barbara Holmes contends that such focused preparations constitute a contemplative stance practiced by Black American communities. She shares the way the labor of Sunday dinner preparations established "spiritual practices that marry full stomachs to piety." Holmes talks about the intimacy of communal kitchen duties that create safe spaces for personal confessions in the midst of difficult life decisions. What is more, Sunday dinner becomes a concrete medium to extend hospitality beyond family to those "down on their luck."

66 Huang, "An Artist and a Citizen."

CHAPTER 4

1 Theaster Gates, "At Town Hall, Nasher Prize Laureate Theaster Gates Pushed Dallas to Build," *D Magazine*, April 9, 2018, accessed August 22, 2022, https://www.dmagazine.com/arts-entertainment/2018/04/at-town-hall-nasher-prize-laureate-theaster-gates-pushed-dallas-to-build/. This quote is from a transcript of Gates's lecture. Perhaps, for Gates, "god" and "holy ghost" are capitalized despite the written transcription?

2 In addition to seeing God's provision for creation in its ability to self-generate (Genesis 1:11), Romans 8:22–23 and Colossians 1:20 also depict its redemption.

3 Theaster Gates, "Web Extra: Theaster Gates," *Chicago Tonight*, December 12, 2012, WTTW, accessed August 22, 2022, http://chicagotonight.wttw.com/2012/12/12/web-extra-theaster-gates.

4 Dependent on God's triune covenantal relationship with humanity, William Dyrness declares that culture can operate as a sanctuary; a place "in which God's glory is made manifest"; William A. Dyrness, *The Earth Is God's: A Theology of American Culture* (Maryknoll, NY: Orbis, 1997), 74.

5 Willie James Jennings, "The Aesthetic Struggle and Ecclesial Vision," in *Black Practical Theology*, ed. Dale B. Andrews and Robert London Smith Jr. (Waco: Baylor University Press, 2015), 182.

6 Anthony Pinn and Benjamin Valentin, "Introduction," in *Ties That Bind: African American and Hispanic/Latino/a Theologies in Dialogue*, ed. Anthony Pinn and Benjamin Valentin (New York: Continuum, 2001), 13.

7 Amy Oden, *And You Welcomed Me: A Sourcebook on Hospitality in Early Christianity* (Nashville: Abingdon Press, 2001), 15.

8 Jessica Klingelfuss, "Theaster Gates Hits All the High Notes in Bristol's Temple Church," *Wallpaper**, October 30, 2015, accessed August 22, 2022, http://www.wallpaper.com/art/theaster-gates-sanctum.

9 Apropos to Gates's exhibition aim, Margaret Miles argues that historical religious images "provide a range and depth for women's history" more so than theological "verbal text"; Margaret Miles, *Image as Insight: Visual Understanding in Western Christianity and Secular Culture* (Eugene, OR: Wipf & Stock, 2006), 10.

10 Alastair Sooke, "The Intriguing History of the 'Black Madonna,'" BBC, July 19, 2018, accessed August 22, 2022, http://www.bbc.com/culture/story/20180719-the-intriguing-history-of-the-black-madonna.

11 Kelly Brown Douglas, "Teaching Womanist Theology," in *Living the Intersection: Womanism and Afrocentrism in Theology*, ed. Cheryl J. Sanders (Minneapolis: Fortress, 1995), 154.

12 Theaster Gates, "Changing Chicago One Block at a Time: Theaster Gates," interview, Windy City Live, May 2, 2016, Chicago: ABC/WLS-TV, accessed August 22, 2022, http://abc7chicago.com/society/changing-chicago-one-block-at-a-time-theaster-gates/1318611/.

13 While playing with a pellet gun at a Cleveland recreation center, Tamir Rice was shot and killed by two police officers. The officers were not indicted; James H. Miller, "Gazebo Where Tamir Rice Was Shot Is Now at Stony Island Arts Bank in Chicago," *The Art Newspaper*, November 21, 2017, accessed August 22, 2022, http://theartnewspaper.com/news/gazebo-where-tamir-rice-was-shot-is-now-at-stony-island-arts-bank-in-chicago.

14 Aja Monet, "Offering," in *My Mother Was a Freedom Fighter* (Chicago: Haymarket Books, 2017), 19.

15 Pinn and Valentin, "Introduction," 48.

16 Raimundo Panikkar, *Worship and Secular Man* (Maryknoll, NY: Orbis, 1973), 24. Panikkar also asserts that the secular sphere is where consciousness evolves in its attempt to grasp humanity. "Only worship can prevent secularization from becoming inhuman, and only secularization can save worship from being meaningless" (1–4). For more on the idea of the shaping influences of secular liturgies, see James K. A. Smith, *Desiring the Kingdom* (Grand Rapids, MI: Baker Books, 2009). On the shaping of Christian desire in regard to aesthetics, see William Dyrness, *Poetic Theology* (Grand Rapids, MI: Eerdmans, 2010).

17 Raimundo Panikkar, *Blessed Simplicity: The Monk as Universal Archetype* (New York: Seabury, 1982), 12.

18 Theaster Gates, "At Town Hall." By the way, this quote is from a transcript of Gates's lecture. Perhaps, then, for Gates, "god" and "holy ghost" are capitalized despite the written interpretation?

19 This is the argument presented by Robert K. Johnston in *God's Wider Presence: Reconsidering General Revelation* (Grand Rapids, MI: Baker Academic, 2014), 13.

20 Theaster Gates, "Artist Talk: Theaster Gates—But to Be a Poor Race," conversation with Hamza Walker, Regen Projects, Los Angeles, January 15, 2017.

21 Grant Kester, *Conversation Pieces: Community and Communication in Modern Art* (Berkeley: University of California Press, 2004), 90.

22 Paul Fiddes's *Freedom and Limit* is one such example. Throughout the dialogical method of this study, Fiddes is adamant in keeping the two fields in adjacent positions like railroad tracks: they travel in a common direction, but they must keep their autonomy and resist overlap; Paul Fiddes, *Freedom and Limit: A Dialogue between Literature and Christian Doctrine* (New York: St. Martin's Press, 1991), 33–34.

23 Emmanuel Levinas, *Ethics as a First Philosophy*, in *The Levinas Reader*, ed. Seán Hand (Oxford: Blackwell, 1989), 82. Levinas adopts Martin Buber's I–thou proposition.

24 Jacques Derrida and Anne Dufourmantelle, *Of Hospitality* (Stanford, CA: Stanford University Press, 2000), 3.

25 Derrida and Dufourmantelle, *Of Hospitality*, 5.

26 Anne Dufourmantelle, "Hospitality—Under Compassion and Violence," in *The Conditions of Hospitality: Ethics, Politics, and Aesthetic on the Threshold of the Possible*, ed. Thomas Claviez (New York: Fordham University Press, 2013), 15, 16.

27 Christine D. Pohl, *Making Room: Recovering Hospitality as a Christian Tradition* (Grand Rapids, MI: Eerdmans, 1999), 22.

28 Cornel West, "On Liberation Theology: Segundo and Hinkelammert," in *The Cornel West Reader* (New York: Basic Civitas Books, 1999), 393. "Liberation theology at its best is a worldly theology—a theology that not only opens our eyes to the social misery of the world, but also teaches us better to understand and transform it" (398).

29 Elizabeth Newman, *Untamed Hospitality: Welcoming God and Other Strangers* (Grand Rapids, MI: Brazos, 2007), 63.

30 Newman, *Untamed Hospitality*, 71. The theologian Catherine Pickstock also comments that the liturgical presents a social ethos that differs from the dispassionate tenor of rationalism. Catherine Pickstock, "Liturgy, Art, and Politics," *Modern Theology* 16, no. 2 (April 2000): 167.

31 *Artsy* webpage, biography notes for Theaster Gates, accessed August 22, 2022, www.artsy.net/artist/theaster-gates?sort=-published_at&utm _medium=email&utm_source=transactional&utm_campaign= personalized_artists_and_artworks.

32 Samuel Solivan, *The Spirit, Pathos and Liberation: Toward an Hispanic Pentecostal Theology* (Sheffield: Sheffield Academic Press, 1998), 12.

33 Barbara Holmes, *Joy Unspeakable: Contemplative Practices of the Black Church* (Minneapolis: Augsburg Fortress, 2004), 5.

34 Holmes, *Joy Unspeakable*, 7.

35 "Theaster Gates and Carolyn Christov-Bakargiev in Conversation," in *Theaster Gates: 12 Ballads for Huguenot House*, dOCUMENTA 13, by Michael Darling et al. (Cologne: Walther Konig, 2012), 15.

36 Samuel Solivan, "Holy Spirit—Personalization and the Affirmation of Diversity," in *Teología en Conjunto: A Collaborative Hispanic Protestant Theology*, ed. José David Rodriquez and Loida I. Martell-Otero (Louisville, KY: Westminster John Knox, 1997), 53.

37 Theaster Gates, "Innovation in Art and Space," interview by Thelma Golden, 2013 Aspen Ideas Festival, Aspen Institute, August 27, 2013, accessed August 22, 2022, https://www.youtube.com/watch?v=6MslDkPsGHg.

38 Willie James Jennings, "The Aesthetic Struggle and Ecclesial Vision," in *Black Practical Theology*, ed. Dale B. Andrews and Robert London Smith Jr. (Waco: Baylor University Press, 2015), 182.

39 Solivan reasons in *The Spirit, Pathos and Liberation*, "correct doctrine does not and has not automatically led to biblically responsible action on behalf of the widow, the poor or the incarcerated" (11).

40 Solivan, *The Spirit, Pathos and Liberation*, 27.

41 Jürgen Moltmann, "Christianity: A Religion of Joy," in *Joy and Human Flourishing: Essays on Theology, Culture, and the Good Life*, ed. Miroslav Volf and Justin Crisp (Minneapolis: Fortress, 2015), 2.

42 Willie James Jennings, "Theology of Joy: Willie James Jennings with Miroslav Volf," video interview, Yale Center for Faith and Culture, August 21, 2014, accessed August 22, 2022, https://www.youtube.com/watch?v=1fKD4Msh3rE.

43 Jennings, "Theology of Joy."

44 Theaster Gates, interview by author, Stony Island Arts Bank, Grand Crossings, Chicago, May 7, 2016.

45 Jennings, "Theology of Joy."

46 Gates, interview by author.

47 Jennings, "Theology of Joy."

48 Jennings, "Theology of Joy."

49 Theaster Gates, "At Town Hall."

50 Jian Ghomeshi, "The Best of Q: Theaster Gates on the Art of Urban Space," CBC Radio, April 24, 2014, accessed August 22, 2022, https://www.cbc.ca/radio/q/schedule-for-thursday-april-24-1.2983113/best-of-q-theaster-gates-on-the-art-of-urban-space-1.2983357.

51 Mackenzie Goldberg, "Watch Theaster Gates Give Moving Speech as He Receives Honorary Doctorate from UAL," Archinect, July 20, 2018, accessed August 22, 2022, https://archinect.com/news/article/150074266/watch-theaster-gates-give-moving-speech-as-he-receives-honorary-doctorate-from-ual. Gates sings the refrain that he prays nightly in his acceptance speech to receive an honorary doctorate degree from the University of Arts London.

Alexander, Estrelda. *Black Fire: One Hundred Years of African American Pentecostalism.* Downers Grove, IL: IVP Academic, 2011.

ArtReview. Power 100, 2019. https://artreview.com/power-100?year=2019.

Bachelard, Gaston. *The Poetics of Space: The Classic Look at How We Experience Intimate Places,* repr. ed. Translated by Maria Jolas. With a new foreword by John R. Stilgoe. Boston: Beacon Press, 1994.

Becker, Carol, Lisa Yun Lee, and Achim Borchardt-Hume. *Theaster Gates.* London: Phaidon, 2015.

Benjamin, Walter. *Illuminations: Essays and Reflections.* New York: Schocken Books, 2007.

Born, Georgina, Eric Lewis, and Will Straw, eds. *Improvisation and Social Aesthetics.* Durham, NC: Duke University Press, 2017.

Bradshaw, Paul F. *Eucharistic Origins,* repr. ed. Eugene, OR: Wipf & Stock, 2012.

———. *The Search for the Origins of Christian Worship.* Oxford: Oxford University Press, 2002.

Braun, Willi. *Feasting and Social Rhetoric in Luke 14.* Cambridge: Cambridge University Press, 1995. Reissue ed. 2005.

Brooks, Daphne. *Bodies in Dissent: Spectacular Performances of Race and Freedom, 1850–1910.* Durham, NC: Duke University Press, 2006.

Brueggemann, Walter. *The Land: Place as Gift, Promise, and Challenge in Biblical Faith,* 2nd ed. Minneapolis: Fortress, 2002.

Colapinto, John. "The Real-Estate Artist." *The New Yorker,* January 20, 2014, 24–31.

Cone, James H. *Black Theology and Black Power,* 20th anniversary ed. San Francisco: HarperSanFrancisco, 1989.

———. *God of the Oppressed,* rev. ed. Maryknoll, NY: Orbis, 1997.

Cooke, Bernard, and Gary Macy. *Christian Symbol and Ritual: An Introduction*. New York: Oxford University Press, 2005.

Copeland, Huey. "Unfinished Business as Usual: African American Artists, New York Museums, and the 1990s." In *Come as You Are: Art of the 1990s*, edited by Alexandra Schwartz, 24–32. Oakland: University of California Press, 2015. Published in association with the Montclair Art Museum.

Cummings, Neil, ed. *Sight Works: Reading Things v. 3*. London: Chance Books, 1993.

Darling, Michael, Matthew Day Jackson, Carolyn Christov-Bakargiev et al. *Theaster Gates: 12 Ballads for Huguenot House*. dOCUMENTA 13. Cologne: Walther König, 2012.

Davis, Ellen. *Scripture, Culture, and Agriculture: An Agrarian Reading of the Bible*. New York: Cambridge University Press, 2009.

De Certeau, Michel. *The Practice of Everyday Life*. Berkeley: University of California Press, 1984.

DeFrantz, Thomas F., and Anita Gonzalez, eds. *Black Performance Theory*. Durham, NC: Duke University Press, 2014.

Deitch, Jeffrey. "Jeffrey Deitch & Theaster Gates: I Believe in Places." The Avant/Garde Diaries, Mercedes-Benz, January 13, 2012. https://www.youtube.com/watch?v=m34aIZG-_JM.

Derrida, Jacques, and Anne Dufourmantelle. *Of Hospitality*. Translated by Rachel Bowlby. Stanford, CA: Stanford University Press, 2000.

Douglas, Kelly Brown. "Teaching Womanist Theology." In *Living the Intersection: Womanism and Afrocentrism in Theology*, edited by Cheryl J. Sanders, 147–56. Minneapolis: Fortress, 1995.

Du Bois, W. E. B. *The Souls of Black Folk*. New York: Dover Publications, 1994.

Duffy, Regis. *Real Presence: Worship, Sacraments, and Commitment*. New York: Harper & Row, 1982.

Dufourmantelle, Anne. "Hospitality—Under Compassion and Violence." In *The Conditions of Hospitality: Ethics, Politics, and Aesthetic on the Threshold of the Possible*, edited by Thomas Claviez, 13–23. New York: Fordham University Press, 2013.

Duneier, Mitchell. *Ghetto: The Invention of a Place, the History of an Idea*. New York: Farrar, Straus, & Giroux, 2016.

Dyrness, William A. *The Earth Is God's: A Theology of American Culture*. Maryknoll, NY: Orbis, 1997. Repr. Eugene, OR: Wipf & Stock, 2004.

———. *Poetic Theology*. Grand Rapids, MI: Eerdmans, 2010.

Fee, Gordon. *The First Epistle to the Corinthians*, rev. ed. NICNT. Grand Rapids, MI: Eerdmans, 2014.

———. *Paul, the Spirit, and the People of God*. Peabody, MA: Hendrickson, 1996.

Fiddes, Paul S. *Freedom and Limit: A Dialogue between Literature and Christian Doctrine*. New York: St. Martin's Press, 1991.

Finkelpearl, Tom. "Interview: Rick Lowe on Designing Project Row Houses." In *Dialogues in Public Art*, edited by Tom Finkelpearl and Vito Acconci, 234–69. Cambridge, MA: MIT Press, 2000.

Furnari, Rachel. "High Spirits: The Artist Theaster Gates Can't Stop Reaching New Heights." *NewCity Art*, March 30, 2010. http://art.newcity .com/2010/03/30/high-spirits-artist-theaster-gates-cant-stop-reaching -new-heights/.

Gates, Theaster. "Artist Talk: Theaster Gates—But to Be a Poor Race." Conversation with Theaster Gates and Hamza Walker. Regen Projects, Los Angeles, January 15, 2017.

———. "At Town Hall, Nasher Prize Laureate Theaster Gates Pushed Dallas to Build." *D Magazine*, April 9, 2018. https://www.dmagazine.com/ arts-entertainment/2018/04/at-town-hall-nasher-prize-laureate- theaster-gates-pushed-dallas-to-build/.

———. "Changing Chicago One Block at a Time: Theaster Gates." Interview. *Windy City Live*, May 2, 2016. Chicago: ABC/WLS-TV. http:// abc7chicago.com/society/changing-chicago-one-block-at-a-time- theaster-gates/1318611/.

———. "Innovation in Art and Space." Interview by Thelma Golden. 2013 Aspen Ideas Festival. Aspen Institute, August 27, 2013. https://www. youtube.com/watch?v=6MslDkPsGHg.

———. "The Making of a Con(temporary) Black Public." Lecture at UChicago Center in Delhi, December 5, 2017. https://www.youtube.com/ watch?v=iu_2AtaTgjo&t=76s.

———. "Theaster Gates 'Chicago,'" Season 8, Art21, September 2016. https:// art21.org/watch/art-in-the-twenty-first-century/s8/theaster-gates- in-chicago-segment/.

———. "Theaster Gates: Soul Food Pavilion." Smart Museum of Art. February 24, 2012. Vimeo. http://vimeo.com/37407879.

———. "Theaster Gates, Talk at Armory 2011." January 7, 2011, https://www. youtube.com/watch?v=V6dDKYAqt8o.

———. "Web Extra: Theaster Gates." *Chicago Tonight*, December 12, 2012. WTTW. http://chicagotonight.wttw.com/2012/12/12/web-extra-theaster-gates.

———. "Working the Public, with Theaster Gates." Interview by Naima J. Keith. California African American Museum. Los Angeles, January 24, 2018.

———. "Yamaguchi Soul Manufacturing Corporation and a Potter Named Dave." Keynote Lecture, NCECA Conference, Milwaukee, WI, September 23, 2014. https://www.youtube.com/watch?v=v_QfJGPP974.

Ghomeshi, Jian. "Best of Q: Theaster Gates on the Art of Urban Space." CBC Radio, April 24, 2014. https://www.cbc.ca/radio/q/schedule-for-thursday-april-24-1.2983113/best-of-q-theaster-gates-on-the-art-of-urban-space-1.2983357.

Goldberg, Mackenzie. "Watch Theaster Gates Give Moving Speech as He Receives Honorary Doctorate from UAL." Archinect. July 20, 2018. https://archinect.com/news/article/150074266/watch-theaster-gates-give-moving-speech-as-he-receives-honorary-doctorate-from-ual.

González, Jennifer A. "Costume: Come as You Aren't." In *Come as You Are: Art of the 1990s*, edited by Alexandra Schwartz, 37. Oakland: University of California Press, 2015.

Harris, Melissa. "South Side Artist's Latest Project: Saving Long-Abandoned Bank—Theaster Gates Trying to Enlist City's Help to Transform Building into Cultural Hub and Library." *Chicago Tribune*, August 5, 2012. https://www.chicagotribune.com/business/ct-xpm-2012-08-05-ct-biz-0805-confidential-theaster-20120805-story.html.

Holmes, Barbara. *Joy Unspeakable: Contemplative Practices of the Black Church*. Minneapolis: Augsburg Fortress, 2004.

hooks, bell. *All About Love: New Visions*. New York: Harper Perennial, 2001.

———. *Yearning: Race, Gender, and Cultural Politics*. Boston: South End Press, 1990.

Hopkins, Dwight. *Being Human: Race, Culture, and Religion*. Minneapolis: Fortress, 2005.

Huang, Kelly. "An Artist and a Citizen." *Art21 Magazine*, October 30, 2009. http://blog.art21.org/2009/10/30/an-artist-and-a-citizen/#.VTl_1mTBzGc.

Inge, John. *A Christian Theology of Place*. Aldershot, UK: Ashgate, 2003.

Jackson, Shannon. *Social Works: Performing Art, Supporting Publics*. New York: Routledge, 2011.

Jacob, Mary Jane. *Grain of Emptiness: Buddhism-Inspired Contemporary Art.* New York: Rubin Museum of Art, 2010.

Jennings, Willie James. "The Aesthetic Struggle and Ecclesial Vision." In *Black Practical Theology*, edited by Dale B. Andrews and Robert London Smith Jr., 163–85. Waco: Baylor University Press, 2015.

———. *The Christian Imagination: Theology and the Origins of Race.* New Haven, CT: Yale University Press, 2010.

———. "Theology of Joy: Willie James Jennings with Miroslav Volf." Video interview. Yale Center for Faith and Culture, August 21, 2014. https://www.youtube.com/watch?v=1fKD4Msh3rE.

John of Damascus, Saint. *Three Treatises on the Divine Images.* Translated by Andrew Louth. Crestwood, NY: St. Vladimir's Seminary Press, 2003.

Johnson, William Courtland. "Trickster on Trial: The Morality of the Brer Rabbit Tales." In *"Ain't Gonna Lay My 'Ligion Down": African American Religion in the South,* edited by Alonzo Johnson and Paul Jersild, 52–71. Columbia: University of South Carolina Press, 1996.

Johnston, Robert K. *God's Wider Presence: Reconsidering General Revelation.* Grand Rapids, MI: Baker Academic, 2014.

Just, Arthur A., Jr. *The Ongoing Feast: Table Fellowship and Eschatology at Emmaus.* Collegeville, MN: Liturgical Press, 1993.

Kester, Grant. *Conversation Pieces: Community and Communication in Modern Art.* Berkeley: University of California Press, 2004.

Klingelfuss, Jessica. "Theaster Gates Hits All the High Notes in Bristol's Temple Church." *Wallpaper**, October 30, 2015. http://www.wallpaper.com/art/theaster-gates-sanctum.

Kwon, Miwon. "The Becoming of a Work of Art: FGT and a Possibility of Renewal, a Chance to Share, a Fragile Truce." In *Felix Gonzalez-Torres,* edited by Julie Ault, 281–314. New York: Steidldangin, 2016.

———. *One Place after Another: Site-Specific Art and Locational Identity.* Cambridge, MA: MIT Press, 2004.

Lefebvre, Henri. *The Production of Space.* Oxford: Blackwell, 1991.

Levinas, Emmanuel. *The Levinas Reader.* Edited by Seán Hand. Oxford: Blackwell, 1989.

Lincoln, C. Eric, and Lawrence Mamiya. *The Black Church in the African American Experience.* Durham, NC: Duke University Press, 1990.

Lints, Richard. *Identity and Idolatry: The Image of God and Its Inversion.* Downers Grove, IL: InterVarsity Press, 2015.

Luard, Honey, ed. *Theaster Gates: My Labor Is My Protest*. London: White Cube, 2013.

McCoy, Richard. "Exploring the Freedom to Re-Present Value: A Discussion with Theaster Gates." *ART21 Magazine*, April 19, 2011. http://blog.art21.org/2011/04/19/no-preservatives-exploring-the-freedom-to-re-present-value-a-discussion-with-theaster-gates/.

McDonough, Tom. "Theaster Gates" [interview]. *BOMB* 130, Winter 2014–2015. http://bombmagazine.org/article/2000073/theaster-gates.

McDonough, William, and Michael Braungart. *Cradle to Cradle: Remaking the Way We Make Things*. New York: North Point Press, 2002.

McDowell, Catherine. *The Image of God in the Garden of Eden*. Winona Lake, IN: Eisenbrauns, 2015.

———. "In the Image of God He Created Them." In *Image of God in an Image Driven Age: Explorations in Theological Anthropology*, edited by Beth Felker Jones and Jeffrey Barbeau, 30–34. Downers Grove, IL: IVP Academic, 2016.

McGowan, Andrew. *Ascetic Eucharists: Food and Drink in Early Christian Ritual Meals*. Oxford: Oxford University Press, 1999.

Miles, Margaret. *Image as Insight: Visual Understanding in Western Christianity and Secular Culture*. Eugene, OR: Wipf & Stock, 2006.

Miller, James H. "Gazebo Where Tamir Rice Was Shot Is Now at Stony Island Arts Bank in Chicago." *The Art Newspaper*, November 21, 2017. http://theartnewspaper.com/news/gazebo-where-tamir-rice-was-shot-is-now-at-stony-island-arts-bank-in-chicago.

Miranda, Carolina. "Artist Theaster Gates on W. E. B. DuBois and What Donald Trump Doesn't Get about Chicago." *Los Angeles Times*, January 27, 2017. http://www.latimes.com/entertainment/arts/miranda/la-et-cam-theaster-gates-regen-projects-20170127-story.html.

Moltmann, Jürgen. "Christianity: A Religion of Joy." In *Joy and Human Flourishing: Essays on Theology, Culture, and the Good Life*, edited by Miroslav Volf and Justin Crisp, 1–16. Minneapolis: Fortress, 2015.

———. *The Spirit of Life: A Universal Affirmation*. Minneapolis, MN: Fortress, 2001.

———. *Theology of Joy*. New York: Harper & Row, 1972.

Monet, Aja. *My Mother Was a Freedom Fighter*. Chicago: Haymarket Books, 2017.

Moten, Fred. *In the Break: Aesthetics of the Black Radical Tradition*. Minneapolis: University of Minnesota Press, 2003.

Nawi, Diana. "Interview with Theaster Gates." *Art Practical*, November 14, 2012. http://www.artpractical.com/feature/interview_with_theaster_gates/.

Nembhard, Jessica Gordon. *Collective Courage: A History of African American Cooperative Economic Thought and Practice*. University Park: Pennsylvania State University Press, 2014.

Newman, Elizabeth. *Untamed Hospitality: Welcoming God and Other Strangers*, annotated ed. Grand Rapids, MI: Brazos, 2007.

Oden, Amy. *And You Welcomed Me: A Sourcebook on Hospitality in Early Christianity*. Nashville: Abingdon Press, 2001.

Owens, John. "Shuttered CHA Complex Gets New Life as Artists' Home." *Chicago Tribune*, November 11, 2014. http://www.chicagotribune.com/news/local/ct-dorchester-collaborative-met-20141111-story.html.

Panikkar, Raimundo. *Blessed Simplicity: The Monk as Universal Archetype*. New York: Seabury, 1982.

———. *Worship and Secular Man*. Maryknoll, NY: Orbis, 1973.

Perkins, John. *Beyond Charity*. Grand Rapids, MI: Baker, 1993.

Pinn, Anthony B., and Benjamin Valentin, eds. *Ties That Bind: African American and Hispanic American/Latino/a Theologies in Dialogue*. New York: Continuum, 2001.

Pohl, Christine D. *Making Room: Recovering Hospitality as a Christian Tradition*. Grand Rapids, MI: Eerdmans, 1999.

Rad, Gerhard von. *Old Testament Theology*, vol. 2. Edinburgh: Oliver & Boyd, 1965.

Rahner, Karl. *Theological Investigations*, vol. 4: *More Recent Writings*. Baltimore: Helicon, 1966.

Reklis, Kathryn. *Theology and the Kinesthetic Imagination: Jonathan Edwards and the Making of Modernity*. Oxford: Oxford University Press, 2014.

Schmemann, Alexander. *For the Life of the World*. Crestwood, NY: St. Vladimir's Seminary Press, 1963.

Skelley, Michael. *The Liturgy of the World: Karl Rahner's Theology of Worship*. Collegeville, MN: Liturgical Press, 1991.

Smith, Dennis Edwin. *From the Symposium to Eucharist*. Minneapolis: Augsburg Press, 2003.

Smith, James K. A. *Desiring the Kingdom*. Grand Rapids, MI: Baker Books, 2009.

Smith, Stephanie, ed. *Feast: Radical Hospitality in Contemporary Art*. Chicago: Smart Museum of Art, University of Chicago, 2013.

Soja, Edward W. *Postmodern Geographies: The Reassertion of Space in Critical Social Theory*, 2nd ed. London: Verso, 2011.

Solivan, Samuel. "Holy Spirit—Personalization and the Affirmation of Diversity." In *Teología en Conjunto: A Collaborative Hispanic Protestant Theology*, edited by José David Rodriquez and Loida I. Martell-Otero, 53. Louisville, KY: Westminster John Knox, 1997.

———. *The Spirit, Pathos and Liberation: Toward an Hispanic Pentecostal Theology.* Sheffield: Sheffield Academic Press, 1998.

Solway, Diane. "The Change Agent." *W* 42, no. 6 (June 2013): 96.

Sooke, Alastair. "The Intriguing History of the 'Black Madonna.'" BBC, July 19, 2018. http://www.bbc.com/culture/story/20180719-the-intriguing -history-of-the-black-madonna.

Sorett, Josef. *Spirit in the Dark: A Religious History of Racial Aesthetics*. New York: Oxford University Press, 2016.

Taylor, Charles. *A Secular Age*. Cambridge, MA: The Belknap Press of Harvard University Press, 2007.

"Theaster Gates: A Way of Working" [conference; various speakers]. Vera List Prize for Art and Politics. The New School, New York, September 18, 2013. http://www.veralistcenter.org/engage/event/1885/theaster-gates-a-way-of-working/.

Thiessen, Gesa Elsbeth, ed. *Theological Aesthetics: A Reader*. Grand Rapids, MI: Eerdmans, 2004.

Thompson, Nato, ed. *Living as Form: Socially Engaged Art from 1991–2011*. New York: MIT Press, 2012.

Todd, Leonard. "Carolina Clay: The Life and Legend of the Slave Potter, Dave." Leonardtod.com. http://leonardtodd.com/daves-poems_284.html.

Vanderwilt, Jeffrey. *A Church without Borders*. Collegeville, MN: Liturgical Press, 1998.

Volf, Miroslav. *Exclusion and Embrace: A Theological Exploration of Identity, Otherness, and Reconciliation*. Nashville: Abingdon, 1996.

"We Broke Down ArtReview's Power 100 by Race, Gender, Profession, and Place of Birth." *Artsy*, October 20, 2016. https://www.artsy.net/article/ artsy-editorial-we-broke-down-the-art-world-s-100-most-powerful-people-by-race-gender-profession-and-place-of-birth.

"We Broke Down ArtReview's Power 100 by Race, Gender, Profession, and Place of Birth." *Artsy*, November 2, 2017. https://www.artsy.net/article/ artsy-editorial-broke-artreviews-power-100-race-gender-profession -place-birth.

Weber, Max. *The Protestant Ethic and the Spirit of Capitalism*. New York: Penguin Classics, 2002.

Wei, Lily. "In the Studio: Theaster Gates." *Art in America* 99, no. 11 (December 2011): 120–27.

Weil, Simone. *Waiting for God*. New York: Harper Torchbooks, 1973.

West, Cornel. "On Liberation Theology: Segundo and Hinkelammert." In *The Cornel West Reader*, 393–400. New York: Basic Civitas Books, 1999.

Williams, Rowan. "Rights, Recognition, and the Body of Christ." Payton Lectures. Fuller Theological Seminary, Pasadena, CA, April 5, 2018.

Wilson, William Julius. *When Work Disappears*. New York: Vintage, 1996.

Wilson Bridges, Flora. *Resurrection Song: African American Spirituality*. Maryknoll, NY: Orbis, 2001.

Wright, Michael. "An Aesthetic of Contemplative Art-Making." Conference lecture, Christians in the Visual Arts, Azusa Pacific University, Azusa, CA, June 17, 2017.

Wright, Michelle. *Becoming Black: Creating Identity in the African Diaspora*. Durham, NC: Duke University Press, 2004.

Yoder, John Howard. *Body Politics*. Scottdale, PA: Herald Press, 2001.

Yong, Amos. *Hospitality and the Other: Pentecost, Christian Practices, and the Neighbor*. Maryknoll, NY: Orbis, 2008.

Zorach, Rebecca. "Art & Soul: An Experimental Friendship between the Street and a Museum." *Art Journal* 70, no. 2 (Summer 2011): 66–87.